Dispatches from a Coup in Progress
Volume One

Voices of the Brazilian Left

Edited by Brian Mier

Design & layout by Daniel Hunt
Illustration by Adriana Galuppo

Contents

ACKNOWLEDGMENTS

I would like to start off by thanking the interviewees. This book would have been impossible without them. I'd like to thank Aline Piva and Liliana Muscarella from the Council on Hemispheric Affairs (COHA) Brazil Research Unit, for valuable feedback and editing and for allowing me to print interviews that originally appeared on their website. Over the course of 2016-2017, I worked as a local producer for Al Jazeera's media show - The Listening Post. In seeking to understand and report on Brazilian media, the team did its best to speak to people on all sides of the political spectrum, and were kind enough to allow us to run the full transcripts from the interviews that I thought were most interesting. For that, I would like to thank Richard Gizbert, Meenakshi Ravi, Paolo Ganino, Will Yong, Hasan Rrahmani, Ziad Elramly and Louisa Gomez. I'd like to thank Dan Beeton from the Center for Economic and Policy Research (CEPR) for publishing the first interview in the book back in 2014 and for giving me the advice to always be vigorous with facts and sources when publishing anything that expresses a left viewpoint, to mitigate the risk of attack from well-funded conservatives.

Bill Goldsmith, from Cornell University, was one of the people who influenced me to move to Brazil in the first place, and has given me valuable feedback on political and economic issues since I first moved down here in 1991. Sharon Mier and John Goldsmith helped with the revisions of early drafts of the manuscript. I'd like to thank Sean Mitchell, who I first met while living in São Luis, Maranhão in 2004 while he was down there conducting research for his excellent book, *Relaunching Alcântara: Space, Race, Technology and Inequality in Brazil*.

Daniel Hunt and I joined forces in 2015, when someone asked me if I was the author of a great article, called *Echoes in the Echo Chamber*, in Brasil Wire. Since then, virtually everything I have written about Brazil has involved bouncing ideas back and forth with Dan. He provided editorial support for this book, designed the cover and laid out the manuscript for publishing. For the past 5 years I have been an irregular correspondent on This is Hell radio show on WNUR in Chicago. The host, Chuck Mertz, continually challenges me with complicated questions that make me think, and this process contributed to the intellectual formation of this book. I'd like to thank my sons Roberto and Jonathan for supporting me on my creative projects in general including this book.

Finally I'd like to thank the Brasil Wire readers for supporting our site, especially the following individuals who donated to this book project: Alexander Jeri, Steve Allene, Jenny Bauer, Carey's Lounge, Stephen Boyd, Holger Beier, Bernardo Van de Schepop, Douglas Graham, Barbara Penning, Carlos Turdera, Mary Adronis, Teresa Meade and Gabriel Deslandes.

To all of you, in the words of Samora Machel:
A *luta continua*!

PREFACE

In August 2014 a project was born out of necessity. In the world's fifth largest nation by population - over 207 million - it had been evident for a year or more that events in the country were not business as usual, and that the coming election, whatever its outcome and consequences, needed to be covered with more context and scope than was then being provided by an international media, which resembled a campaign against the incumbent Dilma Rousseff over the previous eighteen months.

We had seen the hypocrisy on Venezuela, the whitewash of the Paraguayan Coup in 2012, and saw no reason to assume that things would be any different in Brazil.

A failed state narrative here, a questioned mandate there; we saw protest misrepresented, blame mis-apportioned, events weaponized, with over half the voting population infantilized, and shuddered to imagine how the coming election would look through this distorted northern lens. And we were not wrong: "How to back Brazilian regime change" enthused the UK Times, "Dilma should just let the opposition take this one" suggested one US journalist.

A day into the project, a private jet carrying Eduardo Campos crashed near the port city of Santos in the state of São Paulo, killing the presidential candidate. This event left the country in trauma, the election suddenly wide open, and Brasil Wire's founders with added urgency to establish a new and independent English-language platform. It had to be free of corporate and post-colonial influence - be it the kind which runs editorially through most Anglo coverage, or that results from what Arundhati Roy calls the 'Honey-trap' of philanthropic foundation funding.

From the initial small group of founders, Brasil Wire has expanded to over 30 contributors. Scholars, activists, organic intellectuals, bloggers and professional journalists have all joined the project, which regularly publishes 5-10 articles per month and produces video documentary where foreign crews will not or can not go, such as the demonstrations of resistance against the Coup, which were for the most part ignored.

Priorities were to cover the missing elements to Brazil's story, and giving international voice to those ignored by northern media, voices without whom no narrative on the country can make any sense. Through this we hoped to help counter the embedded influence of Wall Street, corporate think-tanks and the State Department itself, on the output of news organizations such as Reuters, Bloomberg and Associated Press, where the neoliberal mantra of 'There is no alternative' resounds as strongly as ever. Their output ranged from blasé group-think to bad faith, censorship and outright dishonesty.

Anecdotally we witnessed first hand the gulf between what journalists would say in private and what could be published, to the extent of threatened dismissal for even using the word Coup to describe what was happening.

As various corrupt and reactionary putschist factions aligned to end Brazil's longest ever period of democratic and economic stability - in the name of a spurious US-led and continent-wide war on corruption - we watched the comprador class, *entreguistas*, what Eduardo Galeano defined as the 'Commission-Agent Bourgeoisie' as they celebrated the protection of their elite privileges over the working class at the cost of their country's discreet re-colonization.

Privatization of natural resources and strategic assets, abolition of labor rights, proposed changes to the pension system which would see many more Brazilians die before retirement, and a twenty year constitutional freeze on health and education investment, were all breathlessly cheered by northern correspondents and news bureaus, with absolute disregard for Brazil's democracy, sovereignty and dignity.

Brazil now enters a crucial period, where a Coup that began immediately after Rousseff's 2014 election victory is being consolidated daily in the erosion of ordinary people's rights and interference in democratic process. It has also gone from a regional power with independent foreign policy to submissive US client state, or neoliberal viceroyalty. How the Brazilian people resist will shape the country for a generation or more.

What is certain, is that history will not be kind to those who pretended that this wasn't happening.

In this book, friend and comrade Brian Mier has compiled a selection of exclusive interviews with important and more often than not overlooked voices of the Brazilian left, from various organizations and positions. It is the beginning of a series which we hope will become useful reference for those seeking to better understand Brazil's contemporary situation.

Daniel Hunt

Editor, Brasil Wire

Introduction

In 2016 a corrupt, conservative Brazilian Congress impeached its first woman president, Dilma Rousseff. There was overwhelming evidence that what had just happened was illegal. Shortly after taking office President Michel Temer gave a speech at AS/COA in New York in which he said that President Rousseff was impeached, not over the official accusations of a non-impeachable infraction called "fiscal peddling", but because she failed to support his party's Washington Consensus-style economic plan. In other words the president himself publicly admitted that the impeachment was a sham. Nevertheless, when Rousseff was removed from office the messages in the Northern media, repeated like mantra, were: the impeachment was a legal process; Brazil's democratic institutions are working; and the Brazilian people have won a victory in the fight against corruption. Immediately after taking office, Michel Temer butchered public health and education spending while raising salaries for the corrupt judiciary that had put him in office by R$57 billion, and shelled an estimated R$1 Trillion in tax abatement out to foreign oil companies. The Northern media cheer-leading continued. As Temer set labor rights back 50 years and his popularity dropped to 4%, a chorus of paid hacks with no formal training in economics from places like The New York Times, Washington Post and Bloomberg gushed a new mantra: he's unpopular, but he's pushing through important economic reforms.

There is no doubt that the so-called "Pink Tide" of radical and center-left governments that spread throughout the region under the George W. Bush administration is being pushed back, supported by international capital and the U.S. government. The rise of ultra-neoliberal governments is a continent-wide phenomenon that is not limited to Brazil and not primarily a result of the "people's frustration with corruption," which seems to be the new U.S. tactic for slandering democratically elected governments with the collapse of moral authority on human rights issues and torture. The current Brazilian government—which is rolling back decades of gains in women's, Afro-Brazilian, environmental, indigenous, small farmers, and labor rights—is more a result of conservatives' inability to win four consecutive democratic presidential elections than any kind of perceived "failure of the left." Illegitimate president Michel Temer's PMDB party (*Partido de Movimento Democratico Brasileiro*, Brazilian Democratic Movement Party) has never actually won a presidential election, taking power three times though impeachments or the sudden death of a president-elect. The fact that it is back in power in Brazil, with an extremely corrupt government, cannot in any way be considered a victory in the fight against corruption.

This book was compiled to add to the small but growing body of work in the English language about the period from 2014 to the present in which Brazil transformed from a growing center-left social welfare state that was making moderate progress in eradicating poverty, reducing inequality, establishing sovereignty on the international stage, and increasing civil rights, to a failed state run according to Washington Consensus principals by a rentier class of criminals. It describes a period in which a lawfare operation run by a US-supported conservative and partisan judiciary paralyzed key sectors of the Brazilian economy causing massive layoffs and tripling the size of the recession, during which the nation dropped from the World's 7th to 13th largest economy. As this happened I grew increasingly frustrated, watching northern commentators feign objectivity while stifling the voices of tens of millions of people who identify with the organized left-members of the poor and working class social movements and labor unions and the organic intellectuals and journalists who support them. Why wasn't anyone talking to them? Based on media coverage one would think that there was nobody left in Brazil supporting the PT party, despite current poll numbers showing that Luiz Inàcio "Lula" da Silva is leading all other 2018 presidential candidates by a 2/1 margin. Although this could be expected from conservative Latin America think tanks such as AS/COA and media outlets like Bloomberg or the Financial Times, it was especially frustrating to see this on the pages of ostensibly progressive publications such as the New York Times, which cited the ultra conservative *Veja* Magazine as an objective source dozens of times in the lead up to last year's Coup. It was frustrating during these past four years living in Brazil to have to constantly explain to our friends and family back home- casual readers who enjoy the progressive reporting on national issues in England and the US in papers such as the New York Times and the Guardian- that the writing on Brazil favored conservatives and bolstered support for an illegal impeachment process under a false posture of objective reporting. One of the people interviewed in this book, *Universidade Estadual do Rio de Janeiro* communications professor João Feres, runs a project in which media bias is quantified through analyzing positive, neutral and negative coverage of key news issues and measuring air time and newspaper coverage of different politicians in the Brazilian corporate media. I have no doubt that if this methodology was applied to the Anglo media during lead up to and aftermath of the 2016 Coup, the results would show a significant conservative coverage bias.

As the northern news narrative shifted from portraying Brazil as a winner to a loser nation, sensationalist stories of violence and corruption began to enter the headlines as if it these issues were completely new and not the result of deeply embedded structural problems that have plagued the country for centuries. In 2014, I grew increasingly frustrated with the way I was being edited and stopped writing for commercial media outlets. I began writing for the only places that I could find that seemed interested in showing what the majority of the Brazilian people thought about what was happening in their country. These venues included the Center for Economic and Policy Research (CEPR), The North American Congress on Latin America (NACLA), The Council on Hemispheric Affairs (COHA) and, importantly, Brasil Wire, which was started by Daniel Hunt to address the same problems with Anglo coverage on Brazil that were troubling me. Most interviews in this book first appeared in these publications. To offset the income loss from writing for non-profits, I began to work freelance in television production and helped produce a series of news stories for Al Jazeera's program, The Listening Post, about Brazil's notoriously biased media oligarchies. The production team made the effort to interview people on with different viewpoints, and Listening Post producer/presenter Richard Gizbert was kind enough to let us use the full transcripts of four of these interviews in this book. During this period I reduced my own analysis and commentary and focused on interviews with key figures of the Brazilian organized left. After all, why listen to me talk about what the poor and working class think about Dilma Rousseff's illegal impeachment when you can hear it from social movement and labor union activists? Why read a Guardian article about urban reform written by a guy with a bachelors degree in journalism who barely speaks Portuguese when you can learn about it from a woman who worked with Paulo Freire in the most progressive big-city government in history? This book, represents the culmination of my attempt to tell the story of what activists and intellectuals on the Brazilian left think about last years Coup. Their stories do not fit in the Northern media narrative. I assume that that is why their voices were ignored.

Brian Mier

The Edge of the Coup

This book opens in 2014, on the eve of the presidential elections. Dilma Rousseff had lost popularity since the 2013 protests but still counted on the support of the vast majority of the working class. But there were growing signs that trouble was in the air. Conservative candidate Aécio Neves, from the *Partido da Social Democracia Brasileira* (Brazilian Social Democratic Party/PSDB), who was subsequently proven to be involved in tens of millions of dollars worth of personal enrichment through bribes paid out by institutions like JBS meat packing company, counted on the support of the Northern media and business class. The New York times ran 7 negative articles about Dilma Rousseff in the week before the elections, some of which were based on misinformation published in *Veja* Magazine, which was later punished for election fraud for illegally lying about Dilma Rousseff's involvement in a supposed corruption scheme. The Times ran a front page article in its Money section entitled "How to Back Brazilian Regime Change". Off the record, one of the top paid foreign correspondents in São Paulo told Brasil Wire, "There's an unwritten understanding among foreign correspondents that the U.S. wants PSDB in power". On the eve of the election I interviewed social movement leader Gegê da Silva about the consequences of a possible Neves victory. In January 2016, two months before Rousseff was provisorially removed from office during the beginning of the impeachment process, I interviewed Central Bank economist Sergio Baierle about the pros and cons of 12 years of PT governments' economic management and the challenges that lay ahead.

Luis Gonzaga "Gegê" da Silva:
"Dilma's loss would be a loss for the world's working class"

By Brian Mier

The *Central de Movimentos Populares* (Popular Movements Central/CMP) was founded in 1993 with support from liberation theology sectors of the Catholic Church as a federation of poor people's social movements representing the poor and working class, homeless people's unions, Afro-Brazilian movements, working class women's groups, squatters movements, indigenous peoples organizations and the LGBT movement. Today, it has hundreds of thousands of members, acts in every state in Brazil, and is an important actor on the Latin American left.

The CMP's Luís "Gegê" Gonzaga da Silva is a former communist resistance fighter who was arrested and tortured during the military dictatorship and helped found the *Partido dos Trabalhadores* (Workers Party/PT) party in São Paulo in 1982. He has remained affiliated with the party ever since, and is one of the leaders of its internal Socialism or Barbarism Caucus. He never held public office, never benefited financially from his status as one of the party founders and has spent the last 30 years organizing mass occupations of homeless families in abandoned buildings in downtown São Paulo. I spoke to him in October, 2014, on the eve of the 2014 presidential elections.

Why do you support Dilma Rousseff?

During the last 12 years the Brazilian working class was able to experiment with better living conditions. It may not be everything that we deserve, but there were 500 years since the European invasion during which we lived off of practically nothing. During this period capitalism made no concessions. In these past 12 years, even if the concessions were small, we can see that the people out in the Northeastern back country are living another moment, a moment less wretched than what they experienced before 2002 when Lula was elected. For us, members of the social movements who have a name to preserve in saying that we are part of the left, it would be very contradictory in this current social context to not support Dilma's candidacy.

I support her because there is a huge Northeastern population scattered across the entire country, in places like São Paulo, Brasilia and Rio, who support Dilma Rousseff unconditionally, and it would be a big contradiction if it were otherwise.

Fernando Henrique Cardoso's presidency was one of the worst experiences in Brazilian history and he is from the same political party that is running against Dilma this Sunday. It will be the worst setback in history if Aécio Neves is elected. Even the most radical left parties, like *Partido Socialismo e Liberdade* (Socialism and Freedom Party/PSOL) and Partido Socialista dos Trabalhadores Unificado (Unified Socialist Workers Party/PSTU) are together with the PT now. They are saying "PSDB never again." They recognize the fact that 8 years of PSDB government nearly sunk our country.

There are some middle class intellectuals and journalists, especially in the U.S. and Northern Europe, who have argued in recent years that the PT is no longer a left party, that it is neoliberal.

Any government in a capitalist country has the task of managing the crisis in capitalism. The only country in the Americas that had a successful revolution is Cuba. But for us, who live in countries that manage the capitalist crisis, elections do not represent a revolution. I don't have a shadow of a doubt that we could have done much more during this 12 years if we didn't have one of the most conservative congresses in history, with the evangelical caucus, the bullet caucus [arms/police/

military] and the ruralist [agribusiness] caucus who are all against the workers. So it was very difficult for Lula or Dilma to enact the kind of reforms they wanted to.

When Dilma went on TV last year after the protests began and tried to implement political reform, her own vice president spoke against it. The Vice President (Michel Temer) publically positioned himself and his party against the reforms. Senator Aécio Neves met with the Brazilian ultra-right to set up a strategy to defeat Dilma if she brought her proposal for a referendum on political reform to Congress. And now when this next group of congressmen takes office it will be even more conservative. The changes in Congress and the Senate are for the worse. I agree that the sustainability of a government cannot happen from the top down; it has to happen through dialogue with the working class. This dialogue could have been deeper, but Lula and Dilma never cut off dialogue with the social movements during the last 12 years. How could a rag picker have addressed Congress? During the last 12 years the rag pickers union sat directly with both presidents many different times in Brasilia. They created a National Negritude Ministry [Secretariat for Promotion of Policies for Racial Equality]. For the first time ever, they created a national Ministry of Women's Rights. So, you can't say that it has been a revolutionary government, but anyone who says that it has been a totally neoliberal government is being inconsequential because during these 12 years you had prostitutes unions, LGBT movements, rag pickers and indigenous groups in the presidential palace and this level of dialogue shows that it was different from Fernando Henrique Cardoso's reign.

Lula and Dilma left us lacking in terms of a full social transformation but this is the result of 500 years of history. You can't change everything in 12 years unless you have a revolution and give back everything the bourgeois has stolen from the poor. Are Lula and Dilma neoliberal? Where is this neoliberalism? If Lula and Dilma are neoliberal what name will you give to Fernando Henrique Cardoso's government? If you are going to call Lula and Dilma neoliberal then the FHC government must have been ultra-right.

Who are some of the groups on the organized, working class left that are supporting Dilma?

One-hundred percent of the MST, CMP, *Central Unica dos Trabalhadores* (Unified Workers Central labor union federation/CUT) and most other labor unions are supporting Dilma. There are people in every union in the country supporting Dilma. There are one or two breaks at the top of some organizations, like the case of the *Força Sindical* (Union Power) labor union federation but most rank and file members of the *Força Sindical* are supporting Dilma.

How has PT changed since 1982 when you helped found the party?

I have been involved with the PT since the days during the dictatorship when we talked about the need for a revolutionary workers' party. I can't say that today's PT is the same party that was created in 1982. All left political parties around the world have changed since their founding. The Brazilian left parties that radicalized, like the PSTU, have a hard time electing one single alderman or state congressman. PSOL has managed to elect a few people, but most of them are also supporting Dilma in the presidential election because they have a full understanding of the setback that will happen with the election of the ultra-right. Any government of Aécio Neves and Marina Silva [who entered his coalition after losing on October 5] will benefit from the hidden policies of the U.S. government and the CIA.

How would you compare the last 12 years of PT government with so called left governments in the North?

I believe that the PT has not sunk to the level of the left parties in France, England and Germany because the working class in those countries has nearly disappeared; you only have small segments that are unable to hold large, coherent protests.

During the protests in 2013, the advance of neo-fascism brought the working class to the streets but we realized that there was another project in mind. Today, I imagine what the working class looks like in England - a minority of people working in the service sector. What is left? During my last visit to Europe I noticed that workers who had a high standard of living are being forced to lower their expectations.

What is going to happen on Sunday?

I hope Dilma wins, because her loss won't just represent a loss for the Brazilian working class; it will be a major loss for the working class in the whole world. Aécio will pull out of the BRICS development bank, which could be a big advance for the working class depending on how it is used. We are proud that we have eradicated hunger and that we no longer have a shortage of doctors in our public health system, and we are sure that Aécio will do everything he can to send the 15,000 Cuban doctors back home if he is elected. People in the U.S. have to know who their government's candidate is. Aécio Neves is the CIA's candidate. I hope he loses, but even if Dilma is re-elected we will have to fight a lot for political reform during the next four years. The people are not free just because Dilma or Lula wins the presidency. The people have slightly better opportunities but we are still a long way off from having any kind of revolution. You may say that a revolution would be bloody but maybe with this, with deaths on both sides, we could manage to really change all of this shit.

Sérgio Baierle:
Crisis Capitalism & Brazil's Economic Realities

By Brian Mier

Sérgio Baierle, 62, is one of the World's leading authorities on Participatory Budgeting, the Brazilian urban planning policy that turns a city's investment budget over to democratic control to its citizens, that has been duplicated in over 1000 cities around the World. He started off providing technical assistence to the Olivia Dutra mayoral administration in Porto Alegre in the late 80s and has traveled around the World providing assistence to mayors offices ever since. During this time he's also worked as an economist for the Brazilian Central bank. In January, 2016, on the eve of the Coup that removed Dilma Rousseff, I spoke with him about the strengths and weaknesses of 13 years of PT party rule in Brazil.

Brazil underwent a transformation during the first period of PT rule that was sparked off by ten years of solid growth. What's happened since then?

First of all I do not think it is possible to say that Brazil had 10 years of solid growth after Lula's election. By any indicator that you use, you will see that the government had its highs and lows. If you look at the GDP you will see there were highs and lows, although it established an average growth level that was higher than the 8 years under Fernando Henrique Cardoso. Furthermore, the process of de-industrialization that was carried over from previous administrations increased (above all in transformation industries). Industry's participation in the GDP fell from 21.6% in 1985 to 10.9% in 2014 (IBGE/FIESP-Bonelli and Pessoa methodology). Agribusiness and the extractive industries (like mining and petroleum) transformed into nearly the only alternatives for growth. The Lula differential can be explained, on the one hand by the commodities boom that was led by China which opened a margin for a group of investments that attempted to overcome logistical bottlenecks (roads, railways, ports, airports, urban mobility, etc), ensure self-sufficiency in petroleum (through offshore pre-salt reserves) and project the country internationally (through the World Cup and Olympics). On the other hand Lula's differential was the strong emphasis on social programs geared towards poverty reduction and increasing the internal consumption market by stimulating demand. This was done by combining programs like the *Bolsa Familia* cash-conditional transfers, Brazil without Misery, which was based on productive integration, and the extension of retirement pensions to autonomous workers who never had formal sector jobs and who were previously excluded. This was strengthened by annual minimum salary increases above inflation levels and financial inclusion policies such as expansion of collateral based credit, greater access to the financial system for poorer citizens and subsidized credit for home-ownership through the *Minha Casa Minha Vida Program*.

What elements of Brazil's economic strategy were carried over from the previous administration?

Lula and Dilma maintained Fernando Henrique Cardoso's macroeconomic tripod: strict inflation goals, primary surplus and a floating exchange rate (semi-floating to be precise). Therefore, the banking and financial sectors' hegemony remained in place throughout the economic conjecture, with monetary stability serving as the base for exchange rate valorization that made industrial rebuilding infeasible and with profit fluctuations remaining at the level of the 1980s (the so-called "lost decade"), notwithstanding the increase in internal demand (for more on profit rates see Michael Roberts' blog article "The Carnaval is over"). It is no coincidence that the current clamor from the business sector is over the wage squeeze, reforming retirement pensions and reduction of social benefits and subsidies.

Reinforcing the power of the hegemonic sector, Brazil remained dependent on foreign investment through the insertion of speculative capital that benefited from the modernization and integration with the great world financial centers. This is what China only recently allowed the financial liberalization that caused trillions of dollars in capital flight. Brazil proudly facilitated this process during the Cardoso government. Totaling the foreign currency generated with commodities exports and external investments, Brazil generated a huge accumulation of dollar reserves (transforming Brazil into the third largest financier of the American public debt trailing only China and Saudi Arabia). Despite the exchange reserves guaranteeing a certain protective cushion during the crises (USA and Europe in 2007-2008; and China now in 2016), there is a high cost in carrying this reserve volume considering the enormous differential in interest rates practiced in Brazil (always in the running for highest interest rates on the planet) and those paid by the US FED's re-numeration of American public debt bonds, which were practically negative until recently.

Give an example of a factor that contributed to the current slowdown?

From 2010-2012, the favorable winds that had been coming from Asia began to progressively weaken. The first pressure came from the financial sector, worried about the Brazilian Central Bank lowering the SELIC rate and the advance of public banks (*Banco do Brazil* and *Caixa Economica Federal*) into the credit market. In 2012 the Central bank gave in and rose the Selic rate preventatively fearing capital flight in case the FED raised its rates, which didn't end up happening. This sign of weakness was passed on to the market. Between 2013 and 2014, Dilma's government decided to put all of its cards into maintaining high demand and returned to programs designed to increase private investments. In addition to increasing funding for the Growth Acceleration Plan, the government decided to bail out large economic groups like the auto industry, for example, with substitution of worker contributions to the pension fund at the value of 20% of their salaries, with a new contribution based on companies gross incomes (with variable percentages between 1.5% and 2.5% according to Federal law 12.546 of 14.12.2011). In exchange for the subsidies the companies promised to maintain their current employment levels. This measure put the pension fund income at risk, further increasing the need of compensatory allocations from the government. Since most of the large companies finance their working capital and investments outside of the banking sector with it's absurd interest rates, they sought out financing subsidized by the *Banco Nacional de Desenvolvimento Econômico e Social* (Brazilian National Social and Economic Development Bank/BNDES). With a progressive elevation of the SELIC rate since 2014 the government increased funding to the BNDES to subsidize this public investment bank's lower interest rates.

This context is necessary to understand the fragility of Lula's style of developmentalism and dramatize the issues currently at stake. While the logistical investments were only partially completed - there are still a series of public works under construction without resources to finish them - the social programs aimed at *what looked like was coming* and hit *what didn't arrive*. According to the FAO, Brazil reduced extreme poverty by 75% between 2001 and 2012, with total poverty reduced by 65%. But Brazil still has 8.4% of its population living in extreme poverty (that is 16 million people living on less than $2/day). The great popular actor in this success story can be found in the so called "fighting class" (see Jessé de Souza: *Os Batalhadores Brazileiros*) which marked its entrance into the mass consumer market as over-exploited autonomous workers working in informal networks, markets, family businesses, pentecostal churches, distance learning courses, etc.

They are the workers who bet on a continual improvement of their lives and that express themselves in the new civilized standards that were achieved in Brazil. Are these real future possibilities or cruel optimism when that that we most strive for is what actually blocks us, such as the structural limits imposed by the absolutism of the market and democracy?

How did Lula's approach differ from that of his predecessors?

Lula's developmentalism, inspired by trade unionism and Keynesianism, tried to reunite in one dream the resuscitation of the nationalist bourgeois of the 20th Century; the base level labor reforms of the 1950s and 1960s; and a new Brazilian miracle with great public investments reminiscent of the military dictatorship policies of the 1970s. This was financed by the export sector (agribusiness and minerals) and financially captured by the ultra-modern and internationally integrated banking sector. The bitter awakening of this clunky platypus reveals a very moderate reformism that is socially and politically demobilizing, immediately threatened by the possibility of an enormous social regression whose symptoms are already being seen in the rapid increase in unemployment and heavy debt hanging over millions of families as cosigned credit transforms into a modern return to debt slavery, as well as the current tendency of collapsing social policies, retirement pensions and public security.

During the 1980s the PT began its ascension to political power through progressive proposals and popular participation in public policy management (participatory budgeting, people's management councils, municipal people's congresses, etc). At that moment it had to deal with very concrete problems that were directly relevant to the needs of the poor and working classes, such as land tenure, sanitation, urban mobility, the popular economy, human rights, local management of public health facilities, education and social assistance. During the Lula government this entire process ended up being reduced to the corporative articulation and hierarchies of national people's conferences. Without trying to minimize the importance of all of the union and social movement mobilization involved with these conferences, today it is possible to say that they ended up being almost entirely put on the back burner during the formation of federal public policies, with rare and very occasional exceptions. It is not surprising, therefore, that the first big recent social protests arose in the large cities over issues related to the use of public space (*Defesa de Alegria* in Porto Alegre) and urban mobility (the fare hike protests of June 2013). The appropriation of investments in housing and infrastructure from the PAC (Federal Growth Acceleration Program) by big businessmen and real estate companies, which was obvious after Lula rifled the Ministry of the Cities off to his allied base in Congress, triggered an intense process of gentrification and real estate speculation with the reproduction, *mutatis mutandis*, of what happened with the national housing bank during the military dictatorship. Contrary to the goal of social inclusion, the end of the division between the formal and informal city, and cohabitation among different classes and sectors, what happened was an increase in evictions that forced the population to the urban periphery, forming pockets of extreme poverty, along with the prohibition of individual survival and income strategies, like street vending, street artists, and unauthorized parties and public protests.

Can you explain how highly publicized corruption scandals like the Lava Jato *investigation are affecting the Brazilian political economy?*

The Mexican drama of judicial and punitive anti corruption fighting caused a much greater problem than that which it proposed to remedy. First of all corruption is not caused by individual failure, even if it results in it. Even 200 Judge Sergio Moro's wouldn't resolve it. Corruption essentially occurs as a form of economic survival within sectors that have low levels of competitiveness or that operate with profit margins insufficient to pay the employed capital. Secondly there is no justice, just administration of justice by all of the powers that act politically, including the judiciary. In this sense the truth and facts are products produced during the mediation between business, the media and public institutions. The infinite prolongation of the *Lava Jato* investigation, for example, has two politically important effects: 1) maintain the government on the ropes, eternally hostage to the new and daily dramatized episodes; and 2) curiously blocking the government to go for the knockout, which would require a restructuring of the forces of the left and right. Since all of the big parties are now in an implied opposing situation, the fact is that it enforces the *status quo*. On the long term, the effect of this false war could be a civil war of the type that nobody remembers anymore. To the contrary of what it appears, the increasing actions by the judiciary as a substitute for a moderating power, previously exercised by the emperor and afterward the military, will not strengthen the state. In the crisis capitalism in which we live, the destructuraliization of the the state and the consequent barbarity is already underway in the peripheries, where earlier they dreamed of springtimes.

What will happen to Brazil in the near future?

Brazil will not end, of course, but Lula's style of reform will. And this will happen in a way that we don't yet comprehend. As Anna Mylaert, director of *Qeu horas ela volta*, said during the 2016 World Social Forum in Porto Alegre, "Brazil is at that moment in which Jessica falls into the pool and Dona Barbara is there yelling: get out of there! Get out of there! But it seems that there is no way back!"

The Impeachment

The following is not an interview, but an article originally written for Brasil Wire by Marie Declerq about her experience watching the historic impeachment vote against Dilma Rousseff in a bar in downtown São Paulo. Declerq, 27, is one of Brazil's best young journalists and a staff writer at Vice Brasil.

April 17, 2016: The Day of Men

Dilma's impeachment is a threat not only to democracy, but to the rights of Brazilian women.

By Marie Declercq

On April 17, 2016 everyone across Brazil glued themselves to the television to watch Congress vote on the impeachment process against PT president Dilma Rousseff. It was a historic moment, not just for the fragile Brazilian democracy that was installed in 1985, but also as one of the few opportunities for Brazilian citizens to watch the Congressmen they elected in 2014 on live TV.

Political polarization was at its highest in São Paulo, the city where I was born and live in to this day. As much as the capital of São Paulo state seems to be a cosmopolitan city with rich cultural diversity, it has a strong tradition of conservatism which still drinks from the fountain of the slavery era. Therefore, the state became one of the epicentres of right wing movements against the federal government since 2014 when they began to exclusively occupy Avenida Paulista, one of the most well-known streets in the city, during their protests.

For the first time in my life as a white, middle class woman with access to private schools, university and a steady job, I felt like a complete stranger in my home town. My friends, workmates and people who were against the impeachment were also tense. We weren't welcome on Avenida Paulista anymore and many people now saw us as great traitors of the Homeland for supporting the PT government.

During the beginning of the voting session in Congress, hearing the angry yells that echoed up the street calling Dilma a "slut", I decided not to stay hidden away at home and to watch the voting downtown where there was a huge concentration of people in favour of the Federal Government.

Sitting in a plastic chair in one of many cheap bars in Anhangabaú Valley, 200 people and I gathered around a single TV to watch each Congressman vote. It was important to note who was around me: men and women of all colours, ages and levels of schooling that believed that, despite all of the shortcomings of the PT government, even with Rousseff's rightward economic swing, she was re-elected with 54 million votes. Democracy was at stake on that day.

And it was worse than we imagined.

Around 5:30 PM, one of the first Congressmen walked up to the microphone to declare his vote. Abel Galinha, of the *Democratas* (Democrats/DEM) party, began to yell words from the National Anthem. "Thou wilt see that a son of thine flees not from battle!... For all the Families in Roraima, my vote is yes for impeachment!"

We watched on TV as the plenary broke into commemoration. The images showed a sea of green and yellow on the streets, applauding and holding up signs that said, "Impeachment now!" On the other side of the TV, the red sea of men and women in front of me with their eyes glued to the TV yelled against it. It was the beginning of Brazil's discovery of the economic interests that supported their congressmen.

The 513 Congressional seats are occupied in their majority by men. Only 45 members of Congress are women, one of the lowest indices in Latin America, meaning we are only represented at 9%. If we break it down further and see how the interests of black women are represented, the number is tiny. What we were presiding over, therefore, was a men's day.

And it was they, the guardians of the traditional Christian Brazilian family, that exercised their domain over the session. The first Congresswoman to appear for voting, Shéridan de Anchieta, from the opposition PSDB, was met with a chorus of, "gorgeous" and "princess" by the men who surrounded the stage. Even in politics, constitutionally elected, Congresswomen are mere decorative accessories.

The concept of "family" was amply used to by many congressmen to justify their votes in favour of the impeachment process. It was similar (if not equal) to what was used in 1964 in favour of the Military Coup. A type of Catholic justification that permeates political decisions in our country.

A few months earlier a Bill passed through this same Congress that aimed to define the concept of "family" in Brazil, ignoring that fact that the Federal Supreme Court officially recognized the stable union of homosexual Couples in 2011. The congressmen from the religious caucus, in clear aversion to families composed of people of the same sex, defined that the only family recognized in this country would be that formed by a man, a woman and their children. This concept doesn't just negate the existence of homo-affective families, but also those headed by single mothers or fathers. Since the first conception of the Brazilian people, this Catholic concept was never observed. The Portuguese colonists immediately adhered to *cunhadismo*, inherited from the Indians, that permitted polygamy and there also wasn't a small number of children who were born as the result of rape.

And it went beyond that. Eduardo Cunha, sitting in the House presidential chair was an official defendant in the Federal Supreme Court for his involvement in the *Petrolão* scandal, as well as innumerable other bribery and embezzlement scandals going back to the 1990s. Cunha, who hides behind Christian morality and the protestors on Paulista Avenue who don't understand they are being used as pawns, is one of the main enemies of women's freedom. One of his most notorious bills, which is still up for vote in Congress, is PL 5056/2013 which aims to make it harder for rape victims to have legal abortions. Disgust with this bill generated positive reactions. The so-called "feminist spring" in Brazil reignited the feminist political movement across the entire country and became one of the main fronts against Cunha in the end of 2015. But on April 17, this didn't matter.

Of the 45 congresswomen, more than half voted against the impeachment. It was there that the difference in treatment from the congressmen flared up. The congresswomen who came up on stage were almost blocked from speaking because of the commotion on the House floor. Those who voted in favor were received with come-ons and those who voted against were loudly booed. One of the congresswomen asked for respect: "I already listened to you, now it's my turn to speak."

My anguish increased when congressman Jair Bolsonaro dedicated his vote to Colonel Brilhante Ustra, a notorious torturer from the military dictatorship era who was known for putting rats in women's vaginas. Bolsonaro, the congressmen with the largest number of votes from Rio de Janeiro, is a known homophobe, racist and misogynist and he didn't hold back from reminding us that Colonel Ustra was the "Terror of Dilma," since he had tortured her in 1970. Bolsonaro generated so much repulsion that PSOL congressman Jean Wyllys, the only openly gay congressman and a supporter of LGBTQ rights, spat on him in a gesture that was only noted after the voting ended.

As if that wasn't enough, Pedro Paulo got up on the microphone to vote in favour of impeachment. Pedro Paulo, while running to become Mayor of Rio de Janeiro, had beaten his wife and demanded that she make a public apology for being the victim of domestic violence.

The votes and macho attitudes of the congressmen hid political giants like Luiza Erundina, Maria do Rosário and Benedita da Silva, who fulfill their solitary mandates in a sea of men who work in favor of their own interests: bullets, bibles and beef.

These congressmen regularly evoke somber times in Brazil. Times when powerful clans worked in favour of the minority that concentrated a great part of the Brazilian income. In addition to voting in favour of their families, two congressmen made a point to bring their son on stage to inform everyone that he would be that political family's next generation in politics.

As we watched the proceedings, the women sitting beside me began to express their worries. Many of them were young, some from Brazil's underserved Northeast, who managed to enter university through the federal government's social programs. For them, defeat for the PT government will mean moving several steps backwards in relation to their late victories for rights. For these women, it is a political act to enter universities and demand better jobs, a contrast to my own privileged position.

I looked at these women who talked among themselves and the men on the TV who voted in favour of the "family." For the first time I saw the face of Catholic hypocrisy in Brazil clearly. These same men who secretly finance the luxury prostitution industry in Brazil are openly against regulations for sex workers. These same men defend their children but don't allow the public schools to teach sex education and don't allow family planning programs. They are the same men who are against the right to abortion even knowing that 1 million clandestine abortions per year happen in this country and that one of the biggest causes of maternal mortality is due to complications from irregular abortions. It is a type of prohibition that most kills poor, young and black women who can't afford a secure procedure to interrupt their pregnancies.

We are the women who are attacked as crazy, whores and abortioners by these illustrious men of April 17. On that date, the Day of Men, we observed a legislative house that does not represent us, that prefers that we stay taciturn and quiet so that they can govern the way they want to. I didn't have the stomach to watch until the end of the voting. When the number hit 2/3 in favor of impeachment, a woman sitting nearby lit a cigarette and, with tears running down her face, I decided to go home. The screams of "Dilma you slut" could be heard filling the streets.

The State of the Brazilian Left

During the lead-up and in the aftermath of last year's overthrow of democratically elected Brazilian president Dilma Rousseff, several writings appeared in progressive English language publications analyzing the state of the Brazilian left. Most of them were written by members of the white middle class, based on little or no contact with the Brazilian organized left which, as Sujatha Fernandes said in a July, 26, 2017 article in NACLA (*What's Left of the Bolivaran Revolution*) is a long-standing problem with Northern analysis on Latin America. One of the purposes of this book is to combat this problem and during the course of 2017 I conducted a series of interviews with working class labor union, social movement leaders and organic intellectuals for the Washington DC based think tank, the Council on Hemispheric Affairs (COHA). The following three interviews originally appeared in COHA in 2017.

Douglas Izzo:
"There is no negotiation whatsoever"

By Brian Mier

On March 15, 2017 an estimated one million Brazilians took to the streets in cities across the country to protest unelected president Michel Temer's proposed retirement reforms which could elevate the retirement age as high as 74. Hundreds of union locals held a one day work stoppage and the teachers' union initiated a national strike. The protest was organized by a coalition of social movements, left political parties and union federations called the *Frente Brasil Popular* (Brazilian Peoples Front/FBP). The largest organization within the FBP is the *Central Ùnica dos Trabalhadores* (Unified Workers Central/ CUT), the country's largest labor union federation and the World's 5th largest labor body, with nearly 8 million members. Arising out of a series of successful strikes during the late 1970s and early 1980s that started in the industrial ABC region of Greater São Paulo and spread nationwide, it is generally attributed as one of the key factors in bringing down the military dictatorship of 1964-1985. What differentiated CUT from other labor federations of the time was its break from communist parties and from dictatorship-recognized unions that were perceived as having a cozy relationship with the corporate sector. Luis Inacio "Lula" da Silva, president of the ABC region metallurgical workers union at the time, had a key role in the strikes and their success led to the formation of the PT party. To this day, CUT membership represents the largest group of base level support for the PT party, and many former CUT officials have gone on to careers in politics. Although the ABC region was partially deindustrialized in the following 34 years it still represents the core region of union activity in Brazil and the São Paulo CUT chapter is the nation's largest, representing around 2 million union workers. Douglas Izzo grew up in Diadema, a poor industrial suburb in the ABC region. He started his career as a metallurgical worker during the 1980s and participated in a series of strikes. In the 1990s he went to college, got a degree in sociology, started teaching and became a teachers' union leader. In 2015 he was elected as president of the São Paulo chapter of CUT. I sat down with him one week before the national protests on March 9 in the São Paulo CUT headquarters to talk about the position of organized labor in the current political environment.

Although CUT represents around 8 million workers today, it was more than twice as large during the 1980s. Why are industrial jobs in decline in Brazil and why has CUT's membership fallen?

The decrease in industrial jobs is a world-wide phenomenon and not something restricted to the Brazilian economy. Important sectors of society became automated. Metallurgical production automated and it takes fewer workers to make an automobile than it did in the 1980s. Around 80 percent of Brazil's financial sector workers are affiliated with our federation and the bank clerks also suffered a massive decline due to automation. It is also important to emphasize that there has been a process of industrial fragmentation in Brazil and in other countries around the world. Companies flee from cities with strong unions and often receive economic incentives to move to places with low levels of union organization where they can pay workers half of what they would receive in the ABC region. São Paulo used to have a much higher contribution to the GDP from industry than it does today. But it diminished considerably while the commercial and service sectors are growing. Another factor is that when CUT arose in the 1980s there were only two national union federations. Today there are 6 official federations plus another four that aren't yet recognized by the National Labor Ministry.

Some American academics and journalists say that the PT party's policies were the primary factor in the drop in Union membership. In your opinion as the spokesperson of 2 million union members in São Paulo, how were Dilma and Lula's performances on labor issues?

It's obvious that the Lula and Dilma administrations were unable to resolve all the contentious labor conflicts in Brazil. But it is also incontestable that during the Lula and Dilma administrations we successfully engaged in a struggle to increase our labor rights. In the current context we are fighting to maintain the rights that we achieved during the past 100 years as they are systematically dismantled. So there is a difference and it is brutal. During the period of Lula's government, the number of strikes decreased somewhat because over 80 percent of our salary campaigns resulted in above-inflation level raises. The monthly minimum wage, which was less than USD $78 when Lula took office, rose to over USD $300 by the time of the Coup against Dilma Rousseff. And back in 2002 the unions were fighting to raise the minimum wage to USD $100/month. So we have to recognize that there were significant advances during this period. In the education sector, where I work, we had large increases in the government's mandatory contribution to the preschool, elementary school and high school systems. The federal government created a national minimum salary for teachers. The national education plan was ratified, mandating that as of 2022, 10 percent of the GDP would be allocated to the public education system using profits from Petrobras' offshore pre-salt oil reserves. There were a series of important advances for the working class but there were still a lot of strikes and conflicts, as much against the Lula and Dilma governments as against PT-controlled state and municipal governments because our federation values union freedom and autonomy in relation to political parties, governments and religion. So we at CUT do not have any problem confronting governments, regardless of what political party is in control and this is how we behaved during 13 years of Dilma and Lula's administrations.

How many strikes did CUT organize during those years?

I can speak for CUT São Paulo, which organizes workers here in this state. There were important strikes against PT Party mayoral administrations. Here in São Paulo City the public workers went on strike against PT mayor Fernando Haddad's administration and the São Paulo City teachers' union held three strikes during his four-year term. São Bernardo was run by PT Mayor Luis Marinho, who was formerly a federal minister and CUT's national president. During his two terms the CUT-affiliated municipal workers' union went on strike 5 times. We also held municipal workers' strikes in other important cities in the ABC region that were governed by the PT party such as Santo André and Maua. And we did this naturally because we separate the relationships we have between the political parties, the governments and the union movement. But it is also important to note that during the 13 years of PT governance over 80 percent of the labor force had annual above-inflation salary increases. Another difference between the current Coup government and previous governments is the way we were treated. During the Lula and Dilma administrations, the government created spaces for dialogue between the business community, the government and the unions to discuss labor and retirement reforms. So before any proposal was ever sent to Congress there was an ample debate among different sectors of society that no longer exists. Today, the government says it wants to negotiate with the union federations but at the same time that government officials give interviews saying they are negotiating with the unions, the Minister of the Interior goes to Congress and says that if any changes whatsoever are made to pension reform they should reject it. So there is no negotiation whatsoever.

How would you respond to the accusations that some people make that the PT party coopted CUT?

The answer is that CUT held numerous strikes against federal, state, and city governments run by the PT party. What our political adversaries, mainly on the left, refuse to admit is that during the Lula and Dilma governments the doors were open for conversation. And when the door is open to talk you don't have to kick it down. Another important point is that there were colleagues who left CUT saying that it sold out who haven't built anything significant. And CUT continues fighting and remains the largest reference of struggle for the Brazilian working class.

The Brazilian media narrative, often echoed in the international media, is that Dilma Rousseff committed a crime and was impeached for it through a legal process. What is CUT's take on last year's events?

The Brazilian constitution stipulates that a mayor, governor or the president can only be impeached if he or she commits a crime of "responsibility". During the Congressional proceedings, the opposition - and this is technical information released by technocrats in the Federal Senate who conducted the investigation - was unable to prove that President Dilma committed any crime of responsibility. If there was no crime of responsibility the judgement was political, not criminal, and therefore constitutes a *Coup d'etat*. The conservatives who conducted the Coup used the means of communication to convince society that the country had been inundated in a sea of corruption. But the deposed government never tried to block or slow down any type of corruption investigation by the federal police. In fact, it created mechanisms to eradicate irregularities of the state. The Lula and Dilma governments restructured the federal police and created mechanisms to monitor and accompany all of the public works projects in Brazil. It is important to note that the new government weakened all of these mechanisms and is trying - and this is something that the Brazilian press is underemphasizing - to destroy the *Lava Jato* investigation. There are leaked phone recordings between high ranking members of Michel Temer's government in which they talk about the importance of ending the *Lava Jato* investigation. Eight of Temer's cabinet ministers resigned over corruption accusations in the last seven months. The latest news from *Lava Jato* is that Temer's Chief of Staff, Eliseu Padilha, received bribes and illegal campaign contributions from the Odebrecht construction company. It is important that people realize that there weren't any allegations against Dilma Rousseff for corruption, illegal financing or bribery. The unelected Coup government is supported by the financial system, the business community, FIESP (*Federação da Industria do Estado do São Paulo*/São Paulo State Industry Federation), the media and the agribusiness caucus and is implementing policies in their interest. It is removing labor rights. The retirement reforms establish that anyone who wants to retire at the age of 65 has to spend 49 years in the workforce. This means unless you start working at 16 and never become unemployed you can no longer retire at 65. This is absurd and represents an attempt to destroy the public retirement system. The congressman in charge of the retirement reforms is financed by Safra, Bradesco and Itaú banks and this reform will end up forcing a lot of workers to purchase private retirement plans from those institutions. No candidate has ever run for the presidency promising to raise the retirement age, end formal employment protection and greatly expand outsourcing. Nobody would ever get elected saying these things. The only way to remove the labor rights that we fought for over the last 100 years was through a Coup and they managed to destroy a lot during their first few months in office.

What is the strategy that CUT is using to fight the Coup?

CUT organized several national protests during the past two years. Yesterday on International Women's Day, for example, we organized a march of over 50,000 women on Paulista Avenue to protest the retirement reforms. It may be that our colleagues in other countries didn't hear about this because there is a communications monopoly in Brazil. Five families decide what content the Brazilian public will see and what information will reach the international news, so maybe our foreign colleagues and even a lot of Brazilians don't know it happened. When unions protest to defend workers' rights, the media doesn't direct one sentence to it. I have today's paper right here - it's *Estado do São Paulo*, one of the nation's largest. [*He holds up the newspaper*] We held a large protest yesterday and you can observe what they are talking about today. The headline is this suspicious football match between Barcelona and PSG (*laughs*). Here's another story about a recent Supreme Court decision. And here is Michel Temer kissing his wife on International Women's Day in Brasilia but there isn't one line about 50,000 women paralyzing downtown São Paulo. And this was a nation-wide protest that took place in every state in the country. This media partiality could lead people outside Brazil to believe that there is no resistance, but we have organized a lot of protests: our May Day protest, our occupation of Praça do Sé, our participation in the Gay Pride Parade. Look at this photo of our protest that put half a million people on Paulista Avenue – look at the size of the crowd in this photo. The media tried to say that it was only 70,000, which is absurd. When the conservatives held their protests the media referred to crowds of 20,000 as 100,000. It called a crowd of 100,000, 1 million – there was this entire process of manipulation. On March 15, we will have a national day of work stoppage and the teachers unions, which are the largest segment in CUT, will start a national strike. Our calendar is full of confrontation and paralyzation, putting pressure on congressmen and the government. I think it is important to emphasize to our friends outside of Brazil that before the 2014 campaign financial reforms it was even easier for large economic groups to elect their representatives to Congress and this created distortion. The big businesses, the bankers and the agribusiness lobby have their own congressional caucuses. Therefore, Congress is not likely to vote in favor of proposals that represent advances for the poor.

Since 2013 we have seen a series of popular protests mischaracterized by the media. The media hijacks the protests and rebrands them for its own purposes— not just the traditional media but forces in the social media as well, like the Movimento Brazil Livre which receives support from the Koch brothers. What good does it do to put 500,000 people on the streets if memes are spammed across Facebook saying that a crowd of 10,000 homeless people marched for free bologna sandwiches? Don't you think that there should be some other tactics beyond street protests to fight the Coup government?

We sponsor debates in city councils, churches, neighborhood associations and all the sites where doors are open to us across the country. We hold these debates to show the dangers of government reforms underway in the National Congress. A second strategy is to build and strengthen alternative media. With our nearly eight million workers nationwide, we have a huge potential to spread news. Our big challenge is to unite our news activities as the right does. If you look at all the big newspapers, they have the same editorial line and the same top stories. If you look at the left media, each one wants to build its own narrative. This does not always contribute to a unified narrative on the Brazilian context. So we have some experiments now, like *Radio Brazil Atual* and the *TVT* Cable TV station, which is the worker's TV station in the ABC region, but they are relatively tiny players in the Brazilian news universe. I think that the alternative media has an important role, *Mídia Ninja* and *Jornalistas Livres* for example, and we try to work together with them to strengthen our narrative and transmit it to society because in Brazil, unlike what you might have in the U.S., there is no such thing as a left or right wing press that offer differing opinions. It's one single narrative, a single editorial position. It is a single voice that greatly influences the Brazilian population to think, for example, that the people who attend one of our protests, taking place on a weekday, are unemployed. It's a deliberate mischaracterization. Because when a protest serves the interests of the media, "My

God, look how beautiful it is. The giant's awakened. How marvelous. It's democracy in action", and so on. And when it doesn't interest them it appears on TV as, "protesters block traffic." It's an issue the Lula and Dilma governments could have done something about but didn't, so we are still stuck with this communication monopoly in the hands of five families who collectively decide what news the people are going to see every day.

Do you believe that there were any foreign interests behind last year's Coup?

We believe that there is North American interventionism in Latin America. It is very clear for us that the old North American strategy to use tanks and bombs has shifted to a more subtle strategy of propaganda, buying political agents and using the means of communication to build movements to destabilize governments using the same narrative everywhere – associating the governments with a sea of corruption. We've seen this happen around the world. This is what happened in Paraguay. This is what happened in Honduras with the Zelaya government. This is what is happening in Venezuela and it's what happened in the Arab Spring when various governments that were against North American interests were deposed. It is important to emphasize the foreign interest in the pre-salt oil reserves behind all of this interference. Until recently, the petroleum reserves were considered a path to the future for the Brazilian people but we see the leaked state department cables that show Senator and former Coup government Foreign Minister José Serra had secret meetings about privatizing the pre-salt with American petroleum corporations. We believe they helped finance the Coup and that they financed destabilization, created agitation through the means of communication and the social networks and built a narrative that manipulated one part of society to impose a de facto Coup against a democratically elected government. This strategy is very clear to us because the same people who were defending ethics and transparency 6 months ago are now trying to bury the *Lava Jato* investigation. This government didn't take power to try to solve Brazil's problems. It took power to guarantee the interests of the North Americans– of North American imperialism and capital and elite interests here in Brazil.

Gilmar Mauro:
MST and the Fight to Change the Brazilian Power Structure

By Brian Mier

During the 1960s, legend has it that governor José Sarney sat down at a table with a group of cattle-ranching cronies and aerial photographs of Maranhão state, in Northeastern Brazil. They marked boundaries on the photos with pencil and divided up the land. In the decades that followed these ranchers committed what Brazilians call *grilhagem:* altering documentation to illegally appropriate land. Sarney and his henchmen fenced off millions of hectares of land then either kicked out the peasants who were living there, forcing them into mud hut settlements between the road and the fences, or kept them on as laborers often paying them with vouchers for use at their own stores and patrolling the grounds with armed guards so that no one could escape. Under Sarney's control, Maranhão state was deforested, and roughly half of its majority Afro-Brazilian and indigenous population migrated to big cities in the Southeast, some of which, like São Paulo, saw their populations increase fivefold over a period of a few decades. The case of José Sarney, who would become the president of Brazil (1985-89) and three-time Senate President, is just one chapter in the 500-year-old story of how large rural landholders dominate Brazilian political and economic life, which is represented today in the largest political caucus in the Brazilian Congress, the *ruralistas,* whose majority recently voted to throw out massive corruption charges against current President Michel Temer.

Unlike other former European colonies in the Americas, Brazil has never implemented agrarian reform. With the world's most unequal land division, 3% of the population owns approximately 2/3 of the arable land. When former president João Goulart attempted to enact agrarian reform in 1964, he was thrown out of office in a U.S.-backed military Coup. As the resulting dictatorship approached its end in the early 1980s, a new peasant-based social movement arose in Rio Grande do Sul state, called the *Movimento de Trabalhadores Rurais Sem Terra* (Landless Rural Worker's Movement, MST). Incorporating theories from liberation theology and intellectuals like Paulo Freire, Marx, and Gramsci into practice, landless rural workers organized in groups to occupy fields of stolen land, resist eviction (sometimes fatally), and farm. Using an innovative organizational structure of upwards and downwards democratic accountability through voluntary assemblies at the family, village, regional, state and national levels, the MST quickly spread across the country and now operates in all 26 Brazilian states, with "Friends of the MST" groups operating worldwide. Although it has yet to reach its goal of enacting agrarian reform and building a socialist society, there are currently 400,000 families living and farming in MST agrarian reform villages across the county and the movement has successfully pressured the government to create a series of innovative policies, such as the *Programa de Aquisição de Alimentos* (Food Acquisition Program/PAA), ratified by former President Lula, which requires all public schools and hospitals in rural areas to purchase all food for their meal programs at subsidized prices from local family farmers.

The MST has a gender-balanced national directorate of 52 individuals, with two people elected periodically in each of its 26 state assemblies. Gilmar Mauro is a member of the national directorate, representing the state of São Paulo. I caught up with him at the MST national secretariat in São Paulo on August, 25th, 2017, to talk about the current political context and its ramifications for the small farmers, who still produce the majority of food consumed in Brazil.

Most food consumed in Brazil is still produced by family farmers. What are some of the challenges that small farmers face

Most of Brazilian agricultural production is, in fact, produced by family farmers, but they are the group most affected by the policy and program cuts that the current Coup government under Michel Temer is enacting. Examples of this include the current lack of access to credit and lack of investment. However, the Brazilian agricultural system was organized to favor exports, especially large-scale agriculture, as part of a strategy to balance the trade deficit in Brazil. Since there is a large deficit in government spending, including servicing the debt, all of the production of commodities in general, whether in agriculture or mining, are geared toward exportation with the goal of obtaining a trade surplus to stabilize the trade balance. So the priority is on large capital, in detriment to the millions of family farmers who survive by producing food. We have to change this. I don't believe that this only holds true for Brazil, but we have a great challenge to change the agricultural production model. The current model poisons the environment and poisons the population. This agricultural production model destroys natural resources and biodiversity. We have to have a debate in society to discuss the role of agrarian reform and the debate should be over, 'what type of food do you want to eat?' and 'how do we want to use our soil, water, and natural resources?' If this is the way that Capital is operating, things will continue the way they are but it will have environmental impacts on this generation and on future ones. If you continue eating these foods from large supermarket chains it will impact your health and that of those who produce it. We also have to return to the debate over technological paradigms and technologies that do not damage the environment and that we can use in agriculture in Brazil and the world, and we think that agro-ecology is an economic and social alternative that is much more sustainable than this model that we are currently living under.

The English-language press – even ostensibly progressive newspapers — has adopted the conservative mainstream language of Brazilian media to describe the MST. For example, I saw a recent Guardian *article which states that the MST "invaded" a few plantations. Why does the MST instead use the word "occupation" to describe these activities?*

"Occupation" is a term that we use because it is related to the large land holdings that were illegally appropriated by various sectors of Brazilian society, including the corrupt politicians who used public money to acquire land, and what is called 'grilhagem,' which involves illegally forging documents to appropriate large land holdings. I can give you a specific example here from São Paulo state. Cutrale, an orange juice producer which also operates in the USA appropriated land that, in 1908 or 1909, was originally earmarked by the federal government for settlements for recently arrived European immigrants. The villages were never built and the lands were illegally appropriated by economic groups that destroyed their natural resources. We use the word 'occupation' to describe appropriating illegally-acquired land that is used by large-scale ranchers and farmers that could and should fulfill its social function. This is the reason that, in our understanding, the challenges against the MST and agrarian reform are very intense. Let me put it into historical context. Our first law regulating land was passed in 1850 and slavery was abolished in 1888. Before 1850, land was public and was farmed with slave labor. In 1850, land became something that could be bought and sold and in 1888 slavery was abolished, bringing freedom to laborers. The slaves did not have money to buy land in Brazil. And differently from what happened in most of the world where agrarian reforms took place as a way to develop capitalism in the countryside (for example, the union between the bourgeoisie and the peasants during the French Revolution to produce raw materials and food for the workers in the cities so that industry could transform agriculture into a market), agrarian reform never happened in Brazil. Brazil started by

53

land distribution into hereditary captaincies; afterward, through large land grants called *sesmarias*, the plantation economy consolidated to its current state in Brazil. For this reason, the struggle for land and agrarian reform is a historical, fundamental battle in Brazil. We organize occupations as a form of pressure toward agrarian reform. There is a law that permits homesteading in Brazil. If land does not fulfill its social function, it qualifies, in theory, for disappropriation. For land to fulfill its social function it has to rationally produce, while respecting the environment and federal labor laws. But most plantation owners and ranchers don't respect the environment or the labor laws and even their unproductive land is rarely redistributed. In other words, we have a historic political problem. This is why we say that the fight for agrarian reform is a fight to change the Brazilian power structure. Brazilian political power is, historically and contemporarily, deeply rooted in the land. Agrarian reform is a way to solve one of our country's historic political problems.

The MST was an important actor in the consolidation of the PT party. The PT's three historic rallying cries were Political Reform, Urban Reform, and Agrarian Reform. With 13 years in power, neither the Lula nor the Rousseff administration managed to push through any of these promises. Why does the MST continue to support ex-president Lula and the PT party?

That is a good question that is related to the Brazilian political struggle. It's true. Agrarian reform did not happen in Brazil. Instead, we have settlement policies. These settlement policies are the result of a lot of struggle and death in the Brazilian countryside. It is a historical problem that the PT did not solve, that nobody has solved in Brazil, and we have to change the political power balance to advance the perspectives for deep agrarian and urban reforms. The MST has always positioned itself in Brazilian politics as an autonomous social movement. It has political autonomy. It is not organically tied to any political party, and we respect all the political parties on the

Brazilian left. But we are living in a context of retrogression in Brazil and the World where forces, not just neoliberal but an entire neo-fascist ideology, are growing as has happened in other historical eras of crisis. We are facing a Coup in Brazil — a political Coup. It is a political Coup that aims to take political power and apply a set of regressive measures to cancel what the working class achieved during recent years, including gains that occurred during the Lula and Dilma governments. Evidently, we did not advance deep structural reforms, but there were important social advances that are now being dismantled [under the current administration]. It's not particular to Brazil. This is happening in various parts of the world because, in our evaluation, there is a prolonged crisis with no way out in the short term. In fact, I don't know if there is a way out of the economic crisis within the capitalist framework. A part of humanity no longer has space in this mode of production. We are confronting power and resisting against setbacks. This is why we are supporting Lula at the moment. We are acting to form resistance, including electing him to the presidency to move forward with social reforms. It's not what we want for Brazilian society, though. We want to move forwards from a perspective of socialism. We defend socialism as a political and economical alternative for humanity, not just for Brazil. Nevertheless, the MST does not have the conditions to do this by itself. The MST is not strong enough to push through agrarian reform. Agrarian reform and changes in the agricultural model depends on a debate within the entire Brazilian working class and changes in the power structure. The MST is an important actor but it is just one actor that is part of a set of actors. Together, we created the *Frente Brasil Popular* (Brazil People's Front, FBP) with a lot of internal differences. But we understand that we have to face common enemies and we have to build a unified political culture. We have a culture of political unity for the Brazilian elections but we do not have a political culture of forming broad fronts for the mid- to long-term. And we are in this process now. I always compare these alliances to a wedding. Two people marry. They are different, even if they have the same gender, but they have common projects and they develop them together. If one person subjugates another in this marriage, neither of them grow and the marriage often dissolves. This is what political alliances are like. Common projects have common objectives and we have to build these objectives collectively. There are static objectives and strategic objectives. Our tactic is to seek alliances with all progressive actors in Brazil and on an international scale to confront the fascist ideology and retrogression. A lot of people fit in this rainbow of alliances and we need to be generous and patient. It's like raising children. I, like a lot of people, have children. We have to say, "Did you bathe yet? Have you cleaned your room?" The left also has to have a historical patience in coalition building. In our point of view nobody has any absolute truth but everyone has goals. We all have ideas and we have to talk about these common ideas to face common enemies. Some may want to overcome the neoliberal order, others may go to the point of confronting the Coup and neo-fascist ideas but don't want to go all the way to socialism. This is a chapter that we will discuss and debate as the process unfolds, but not by searching for hegemony or allowing ourselves to be hemegonized by others. For this reason, the PT is our ally, the CUT labor federation is our ally, the people's social movements in Brazil are our allies and the other left political parties are also our allies at this moment in history.

The largest general strike in many years took place on April 28. The following month there was a huge protest in Brasilia, the largest in that city's history. At that moment it looked like the fight against the Coup government was picking up momentum. The second general strike, despite being effective in some cities like Belo Horizonte and Brasilia, was not as large as the first one. And the night that the corruption allegations against Michel Temer were thrown out by Congress there were not very many street protests. It looks like the organized left is losing force at the moment. Is this analysis correct? What are the

This, perhaps, is the central issue for us and for the whole world. There is a structural problem. Sometimes the left focuses on ideological differences that clearly exist — cooptation of sectors of the left can't be overlooked either because it exists — but it forgets a structural problem that is going on in the world. There is a process within the capitalist productive structure that is changing in the entire world. The productive structurization that started in the 1950s and 1960s is changing due to new technologies and materials that are used today. The Fordist production model created large amounts of stock, used the logic of the production line and permanently produced cyclical crises of overproduction. This has changed in the whole world in part through use of the Toyota production model, which is being perfected around the world. I can't go too far into this because my answer would become very long and complex but we are at a time in history when the world's largest taxi company doesn't own a single taxi. The largest hotel company doesn't own a room. Large businesses no longer have formal employees. This process of weakening and outsourcing in the workplace is a reality for the entire world. Why am I saying this? Because this impacts the working class' organizational instruments. It was one thing to hold a strike during the days of the Fordist model. If you shut down one sector of a factory it would completely freeze the others. Today many sectors are connected from a labor and financial standpoint. Companies centralize some of their activities and outsource others to various locations around the World. Many workers are now autonomous, without any labor rights whatsoever. So the instrument of the strike, which was fundamental to the working class for a long time, is no longer possible in many sectors of the economy. Many autonomous workers cannot strike because if they stop producing they stop receiving and they don't have any financial or physical security. So we have a fundamental question here, from my point of view, and we are debating this within the left. The tools that the working class produced throughout history are not enough to confront the current political problems because they are, generally speaking, defensive measures. They were produced in a specific time in history when capitalist development still allowed advances for the working class. We are entering a new phase in history in which capitalist development is producing setbacks for the working class and it is hard to launch an offensive against this model. It is affecting the union movement. Look at the metallurgical workers in São Paulo's ABC region, who formed the basis for the birth of the PT party. During the 1960s there was a huge number of metallurgical workers in the region. Today there are 13,000 metallurgical workers in the ABC. During the 1960s and 1970s there were 90,000. And today, with 13,000, they produce a lot more than they did back then. The odds are that this number of metallurgical workers is not going to go up, it will diminish. You can say the same thing about the bank tellers, who suffered huge layoffs during the process of computerization, and all of the other sectors of the working class. This has an impact on the working class' political struggle. Is this the only justification? No, but it is a challenge to build new forms of working class organization and representation, to form a dialogue with the working class where it lives, that incorporates location and integrates regions in ways that enable effective confrontation. I will take a second here to talk about a few mistakes made by the left. One of them was to separate the economic and political struggles. Delegating the economic struggle to the social and labor movements and the political struggle to the Party was a serious mistake. The social and union movements ended up falling into corporatism and economics, and the Party disconnected from the people's daily lives and turned into a bureaucracy. You cannot separate economic struggle from political struggle. The economic struggle is also a political struggle because you can't separate the present from the future. We are engaged in an important confrontation at the moment but we have to plant what we want in the future now. I will use agriculture to explain this. If you want to harvest avocados, you have to plant an avocado tree. There is no other way to do it. So, if we want a more just society with more solidarity, we have to plant solidarity here and now. If we want a society in which men and women participate equally we have to open up spaces of equality here now, including inside our own homes. If we want a new type of society with new values, we have to cultivate and produce these values in the hearts of our organizations here and now. Since theory cannot be separated from practice, it should develop like this: new movements have to be built and have to incorporate this concrete economic struggle in a manner that engages with people's daily lives. An organization that does not respond to the concrete needs of its base doesn't have a reason to exist. Concrete needs have to be integrated to the needs of the political struggle. Conversations about daily life, connected to survival, have to be integrated with dialogues about what kind of society we want in the future. These are the challenges that are out there. But to finish my answer to the question — fine, if we don't have these new instruments should we throw everything that the workers ever produced in the garbage? No, because we produced the best that we could. Nevertheless, these instruments are not strong enough to overcome all of the challenges of the moment. We have to modify these instruments and produce new instruments to meet new challenges. Some sectors of the left want to build a new reference point in the masses by passing over historically constructed instruments and tactics. It's obvious that you have to be critical, but you do not build an instrument of popular reference by annihilating another instrument. This is the old problem of vanguardism on the left. Many sectors in the left commemorate the defeat of other left sectors. This is not revolutionary, this is anti-revolutionary. Because new instruments should not be created through the destruction of other instruments, even if they are full of problems and limitations. Whoever has no problems can throw the first stone. Therefore, you have to be humble and understand that we are all individually weak and even while uniting the entire left we are still losing the battle. We are being defeated. So we have to understand that there are a lot of challenges ahead to organize the working class, most of which did not join the Brazilian political struggles. We do have a working class militancy that has been very important. If we hadn't taken it to the streets the Coup would have consolidated to destroy the Brazilian left and we are resisting. But this is still too small to oppose this entire offensive by big Capital in Brazil. I think the situation is beginning to change, though; there is a politicization process underway in Brazil and I hope that we will have historic patience, while at the same time initiatives to increase people's participation, to not always speak to the same people, to modify methods within the left, within our organizations that enable dialogue with the Brazilian people, the working class to, first, understand this moment in history and second, to mount a people's offense to defeat the Coup government in Brazil.

The political conjuncture in the United States at the moment is very bad, and there is a growing so-called "alt-right," with fascism and neo-nazism on the rise, even in the White House. Some people are aligning themselves with the Antifa movement working against these trends. Is there anything you would like to say to the people fighting against fascism in the United States?

Fascism is a danger to humanity and it's not like we don't see it down here. We deeply understand it. In all historic times of crisis alternatives appear, like war, but there is a contradiction. Crises are propitious moments for debate about systems and their contradictions. It is a conducive moment for political debate but during crisis retrogressive ideas like fascism always arise and they have to be fought. All sectors have to come together to fight this. This isn't even a question of ideology. If you are human you have to fight fascism and its retrogressive ideas and everyone has to unite. It doesn't interest me who is at the forefront, who is behind or who is on the side, but all sectors have to unite to face this. This implies that a degree of generosity and patience is needed. And I believe that the U.S. working class is going to face this and will be victorious, just as we will be here in Brazil and other parts of the world. One of our challenges is how we can unite internationally. It's not enough to struggle just in Brazil, but it has to be done in Brazil just as it has to be done in the United States and every part of the world. We need local actions but they have to connect to struggles across the entire world. We have to confront these fascist ideas and face the retrogression with the goal of producing new ideas for the world. We need new ideas for economic and social sustainability, to solve the problems of hunger and extreme poverty and to think about what kind of world we need to suit the generations that come after us. I wish lots of successful struggle and lots of luck to you in the United States. And, look, you have a fundamental role. The struggles in the United States have a fundamental role for Brazil and for the entire world. We support you and we believe that you will be able to effectively face the biggest corporations that practically dominate the entire planet. You can always count on our solidarity.

Erminia Maricato:
Overcoming Deep Inequality in Brazilian Cities

Erminia Maricato is one of Brazil's most renowned urban planners. Author of 11 books and 40 book chapters, her lectures, often in public forums and protests, regularly draw large crowds of young people. But she is not merely an academic. Maricato was a key player in four of the most important moments in the last 30 years of Brazilian urban reform.

Maricato was an actor in the movement that created and ratified, through popular petition, articles 182 and 183 of the 1988 Brazilian Constitution. These articles declare that the social function of property overrides the profit motive and set guidelines for radical urban reform. From 1989-1992, Maricato served as São Paulo's Secretary of Housing and Urban Development within one of the most progressive big-city governments of all time, working alongside Education Secretary Paulo Freire. In this position, Maricato helped create innovative policies to provide technical support for urban social movements to appropriate abandoned buildings and vacant land and convert them to self-managed social housing in accordance with the constitution — policies that were later replicated in hundreds of cities across Brazil. She was active in helping create and ratify the landmark Statute of the City in 2001, which creates guidelines for adherence to constitutional articles 182 and 183 and mandates that every city with a population over 20,000 has to facilitate a regular participatory development plan with full budget transparency. From 2003 to 2005, while serving under former Porto Alegre Mayor Olivio Dutra in the Federal Ministry of Cities, Maricato acted as the technical coordinator of President Lula's national urban development policy.

In March, 2017, a progressive coalition of labor unions, social movements, student groups, and academic and professional associations called the *Frente Brasil Popular* brought one million people onto the streets in scores of cities across Brazil to protest illegitimate president Michel Temer's neoliberal pension and labor reforms. On April 28, *Frente Brasil Popular* was a key actor in the General Strike, which ground Brazil to a halt. At 70 years old, Maricato is coordinating participatory processes to develop the FBP's urban strategy, something she says is for the mid to long term, as "we have some tough times ahead of us." I interviewed Maricato in her home in São Paulo's Pinheiros neighborhood on April 7, 2017.

What was PT's model of urban governance during the time you worked with Mayor Luiza Erundina in São Paulo and how do you think this differs from the strategies used by the government of Fernando Haddad [Mayor of São Paulo, 2012-2016]?

During the recuperation of democracy after the military dictatorship, the social forces in Brazil that were academic, labor, professional and social movements, built a proposal that we called "urban reform." When the Worker's Party took over the São Paulo mayor's office we had a platform that had been collectively built with the social movements. As we recuperated democracy in Brazil, several political parties and labor union federations sprung up as well as the *Central de Movimentos Populares* (People's Movements Central/CMP). We won some mayoral elections together and we started what I call a "virtuous cycle" of urban policy. A large part of it was based on direct democracy. I think the most important program of this period was participatory budgeting. We were living in a period of low investment — there was no money. It was a period of crisis and IMF structural adjustments. We didn't have many resources for public policies, but we deliberated democratically on the allocation of what resources we did have. In addition to participatory budgeting, we created a housing policy that generated a lot of positive results based on technical support from architects, engineers and social workers, so that the social movements could build their own houses. The mayor's office donated the land and provided financing. This was one of our most successful programs and there is a legacy in that it has been continued in cities across Brazil up to this day. We also started a very important strategy of urbanization in precarious areas and *favelas*.

The working class and poor city is ignored and forgotten by public policy during the usual governments. We looked at this forgotten, informal and illegal city, lacking in urban services and equipment and understood that this was our priority. We used a term to describe our strategy, 'inversion of priorities.' During part of the 1980's and all of the 1990's, we had mayor's offices with these inverted priorities across Brazil. These mayoral administrations inverted priorities and facilitated participatory processes to deliberate on policy and resource allocation. Lula served two terms and was followed by President Dilma Rousseff. The truth is — and I've written about this — urban policy changed a lot during these times. My main thesis for why it changed is because money appeared. Public resources appeared. It arrived through the PAC Growth Acceleration Program and through *Minha Casa Minha Vida* (the My House, My Life public housing program). So we entered the 21th Century with the new concept that the Federal Government had resources and was going to invest in cities. When the resources began to arrive our virtuous, participatory project lost space. It lost space because Capital began to take over urban policy. It was a change in the power dynamic — this is very important to understand because it's not just a case of condemning political parties or social movements which, in fact, institutionalized considerably during this period. There was a change in the power relationship that had supported city governments and that was much more democratic and participatory. When resources returned, Capital — the big construction companies and the real estate coalitions — gained space and began to take over urban policy. This is what I show in my last two books. The virtuous cycle entered in decline, although some mayoral administrations continued to urbanize favelas by investing in mobility through construction of express bus corridors (which is a lot cheaper than investing in subways), prioritizing collective transport and housing through technical assistance to social movements. There were some governments in the 21st Century that continued to implement virtuous cycle policies but the fact is that we see that the real estate market and public works were prioritized and this was not the most important thing for social needs. We also had the World Cup cycle, which built a lot of stadiums that weren't a priority.

During the Luiza Erundina administration we tried to make a pact with the business community and it had a hard time accepting us - it was even harder for the media. We have a very unequal society in Brazil and we have very high segregation levels in our cities. When you compare the elite part of the city to the part where the workers live you see that the workers are mainly black, have low income levels, low education levels and suffer from high crime, much higher levels of mosquito borne illnesses and much lower life expectancy. We have an extremely strong division between the people's city and the elite city. We had interesting dialogues about this with the Brazilian business community, both before and during the coalition politics era of *Lulismo* but this has now disappeared. The idea that you could invest in areas that do not make up part of this ideological representation of the city, which is a kind of visiting room for white people with money, is very difficult these days and only possible through a very advanced power coalition. Around 30% of the households in Brazilian metropoles are headed by women and the great majority of these families live on the periphery. A large part of these women work in the domestic service sector in this white, middle and upper income city. At the height of our urban reform movement we fought for and built a new federal constitution that is very democratic. We fought for and built a legal framework that was absolutely new, through measures like the Statute of the City, new sanitation and urban mobility legislation and the Statute of the Metropolis. We were able to build an innovative legal framework but it did not end up being implemented in very many places. This is a very Brazilian phenomenon — there are advanced laws but the legislation is applied in a discriminatory fashion. We have a conservative judiciary which treats part of the city as illegal and this is where the poor people live. It is a population that lives in informality in a part of the city that has no urbanization. During PT city governments and some progressive administrations by the *Partido Democrático Trabalhista* (Democratic Labor Party/PDT) and *Partido Comunista do Brazil* (Brazilian Communist Party/PC do B) we radically focused on this segregated, excluded part of the population.

When Fernando Haddad was elected in São Paulo (in 2012) this socially constructed virtuous cycle project had been in decline for a long time. He took over a government that was supported by a coalition of capitalist forces from the infrastructure and construction sector, the corporate real estate sector and real estate financial capital that had set up a project for the city during the previous administrations of José Serra and Gilberto Kassab. This project was made through PPP's (Public and Private Partnerships) and urban renewal projects and was called *Arco do Futuro* (arch of the future). These conservative governments opened space for the capitalists to organize and propose their project for the city. However, I think that the innovation that Fernando Haddad brought was to open the city of the wealthy whites — let's call it this — the area that the current mayor of São Paulo [former Brazilian "Apprentice" star João Doria] calls "the beautiful city," which is a kind of metropolitan closed condominium. Haddad democratized its public spaces by penalizing the circulation of automobiles in favor of pedestrian and bicycle traffic and by favoring collective transport and lowering automobile speed limits. In other words, he innovated in relation to the progressive agenda from the 1980's and 1990's that we built during our fight against the military dictatorship that we wrote into the new constitution. Unfortunately, he sided with the conservatives on housing issues for the first three years of his mandate because of the *Lulismo* coalition and class alliances and his housing policy only began to flourish with democratic policies during his last year in office. But his participatory master development plan was interesting, especially because it enabled the return of the municipal rural zone and provided great innovation through its food security and nutritional policy. In short, he introduced some new things to our old agenda.

In 2011, Perry Anderson wrote an article called "Lula's Brazil" which, perhaps inadvertently, influenced some progressives to view President Lula as a traitor to the left. In this article, Anderson says that when Lula took office, he immediately adapted a neoliberal policy platform and implies that he increased social spending as a political defense strategy after a corruption scandal broke in 2005. Anderson fails to mention that Lula inherited a government in which IMF conditionalities prohibited increases in health and education spending and that he increased this immediately after the loans were liquidated. He also fails to mention the innovative democracy deepening policies that were implemented the first year Lula took office such as the creation of the Ministry of Cities in which a voluntary, democratically-elected delegate and council system with majority representation from the poor and working class gained a significant degree of deliberative power over the federal urban policy budget. You were the Executive Secretary of the Ministry of the Cities during this period. What was the initial goal of the Ministry of the Cities, what changed, and why did it end up losing power by the end of the Dilma Rousseff administration?

The Ministry of Cities project was born in Lula's think tank, *Instituto Cidadania*, before he was elected. I had left the PT party at the time because I was unhappy with a few things related to historic commitments, but when Lula invited me to create this project I felt that it was important for us to work on a nation-wide proposal. I was very critical of Fernando Henrique Cardoso's policies. There were some interesting people inside of the Urban Development Secretariat but, without any doubt whatsoever, he followed the Washington Consensus. Lula maintained an ambiguous posture between financial sector interests, the traditional interests of the large land owners and the interests of the working class. Lula bet on a national bourgeoisie that doesn't exist anymore. This is the national bourgeoisie that suffered setbacks and started to either disappear or internationalize during the Collor and Fernando Henrique Cardoso administrations. Lula bet on a policy of rebuilding Brazilian industry that now, with the *Lava Jato* investigation and the resurgence of neoliberalism, has started to receive fatal blows. This is because the strong nationalists that we had until recently were the big businessmen and the petroleum sector which strengthened the shipbuilding industry and the shipyards. Lula bet on ECLAC's historic proposal for Latin America, which was rooted in Celso Furtado's strategy to strengthen the internal market by increasing salaries. In my opinion, this was the most important thing he did. Lula increased the minimum salary and redistributed income through the *Bolsa Familia* program. He caused a huge increase in the number of working class and poor students in the university system through the *PROUNI* program. *Luz para Todos* (Light for Everyone) got everyone onto the electrical grid. These were important but the fact is that Lula operated ambiguously by not openly opposing financial and landowning elites while, at the same time, favoring the workers. Lula still thinks this way to this day — that there is no solution through confrontation in Brazil. If we consider that we have suffered from a process of deindustrialization for the last 30 years I think that he could have a point but do not agree with this posture of non-confrontation. And I am not the only one who doesn't agree with it. When Perry Anderson wrote that article about Lula, he based it mainly on the works of Francisco Oliveira, a Brazilian intellectual who broke with Lula during the first years of his government and became a very strong critic.

I was invited to create the Ministry of the Cities and I encountered difficulties within the government. This is something I'd already experienced in the past. You are in a coalition and sometimes you have disputes within the same party. Some disputes are out of vanity or egos and some disputes are political. In the beginning of the Lula government there was an internal dispute with the Ministry of the Cities under Olivio Dutra and our exceptional team. It was such a good team that our sanitation department managed to hold a meeting with the IMF and convince them to free up resources that were blocked through the conditionality agreement. The IMF agreed to free up R$3 billion Brazilian, which was a lot in 2003, for investment in sewage treatment. Why? Because this marvelous Ministry of the Cities team convinced the IMF that the application of funds for sanitation is not an expenditure, as the IMF accounting section treated it at the time, but an investment. It is an investment because you lower disease rates, increase the quality of life and improve the populations' health and this decreases public health expenditure. I'll never forget this. But there was a lot of conflict within the government. At that time, even during the Lula Government, the Minister of the Treasury was in favor of the structural adjustments. When we discussed sanitation there were people inside the government arguing in favor of privatization, which we opposed. The moment when the more democratic sectors lost power was during the *Mensalão* scandal in 2005. That is when the power relationship shifted and the government started expanding the alliances that had started with parties from the democratic, progressive left. When the *Mensalão* scandal broke, the Ministry of the Cities was handed over to an absolutely conservative political party [*Partido Progressista*/Progressive Party], which was known for a series of corruption charges. It was a party that was tied to the construction industry. So at that moment I left the PT and returned to teaching. It was clear that the cycle of democratic urban policy with direct democracy and an inversion of priorities which started in the 1980s was ending. But this wasn't yet clear to the social movements because they still believed in the national citizens' council we created within the Ministry of the Cities.

The idea was that all of the urban policies would pass through this big council that was made up of councilors who were elected at the National Cities' Conference. The National Cities Conference was a huge national meeting that originated in the municipalities. The municipalities had conferences where delegates were elected to represent them at the state conferences. The state conferences elected delegates who went to the National Cities Conference, and there they elected the National Cities' Councilors. It seemed perfect from the point of view of popular, democratic participation. But more and more I think that these local leaders and social movements also took the path towards institutional space. They abandoned a political strategy that was more based on the ground, on the streets, in the factories, the neighborhoods, the schools, the hospitals where we started from. We started on the periphery out in the neighborhoods, in the churches together with liberation theology where we talked about public transportation, quality of life, public health and woman's rights and we started pulling away from all of that.

The income distribution and job creation policies in the Lula government were exceptional. There is absolutely no way that they can be belittled. But from the point of view of political action I think that there was a cushioning of the transformative capacity to advance emancipation of the poor. I say this especially about the black population, which is very, very, very discriminated against in Brazil and especially about women heads of households.

There is a perception propagated in the international media that what happened last year was not a Coup because it was a legal process. What is your opinion on this?

There is no doubt whatsoever that what happened in Brazil was a Coup. Corruption fighting was used as a tool to create what we call a justice party, made up of the judiciary, the supreme court, the media and the public prosecutor's office. Together, they are behaving like a political party that defends the interests of the upper middle class. They began to build this idea that there was never as much corruption as there was during the PT governments. Was there corruption? Yes, without a doubt. Because the coalition — President Dilma mentioned this recently — started with five political parties during Lula's first term. During his second term the size of the coalition increased. During Dilma's first term the number of parties increased. In her second term it increased even further and as the power dynamic changed, they incorporated the parties that now form the base of Temer's corrupt government today. So these corrupt parties that are running Brazil were part of Dilma's government. But now we can all see that corruption was used as an excuse to hold a Coup. We are seeing now that corruption is fully integrated into this new government. This is clear in the accusations coming out from the Lava Jato investigation which affect every major political party. The problem is that the corruption fighting is prioritizing only one of these parties, the PT. As someone who left the PT years ago and has no party ties, I can clearly affirm that this is persecution. You cannot have justice with persecution against one predetermined political party. *Lava Jato* could change Brazil and it would be very important if it did. The big construction businesses in Brazil have been corrupt since the days of the Military Dictatorship. We have doctoral dissertations and master's theses that show this. My doctoral dissertation was about the military regime's housing policy. If we could free ourselves from shady cost overruns in public construction projects, it would be a revolution. If we could free ourselves from illegal campaign financing it would be a revolution in Brazil. But this is not what is happening, unfortunately. What is happening is injustice and political persecution.

What are you doing to fight against the retrogression in terms of urban reform perpetrated by this Coup government?

When I left the government in 2005, I entered civil society and started working a lot on the idea of re-thinking urban reform. At first, I did this in an isolated fashion but today we are thinking and talking about a new project for Brazil because the developmentalist project cycle that was created by ECLAC, based on national industrialization and creation of an internal market has ended. The *Frente Brasil Popular,* which unites sectors of the progressive left, is discussing a new project for Brazil. They invited me to coordinate the urban policy component and we've already started. Professor Karina Leitão and I, together with the National Architects Federation, Engineers Unions, The Brazilian Architecture Institute, and youth groups like *Levante Popular de Juventude (the People's Youth Uprising social movement)* and the UNE (*União Nacional de Estudantes/*National Student's Union) are discussing a new project for Brazilian cities. This is not a short-term project. I see some very difficult times ahead of us on the short term. I've been traveling around Brazil and hunger, which we haven't seen since Lula was first elected, is returning to the urban peripheries. Unemployment is deepening. Violence is getting worse. The homicide rate is going up. So I think we have to prepare for very hard times in the next few years. But we are building a new project for the country for the mid and long term. Brazil will change. It has a future. It is a very big, rich country from a natural resources standpoint with 200 million inhabitants. It will definitely recuperate and I think that the earlier we have a proposal together and we are able to open space for this recuperation to happen democratically, the better. This process can definitively break with hundreds of years of slavery, because we haven't fully broken from our past. And this is why we are developing a civil society project now. I'm 70 and I want to dedicate what life I still have to a proposal for social construction — not just construction of a governmental project on paper. I've already done that. I want to work on a program for Brazilian society so that we can overcome this very deep and cruel inequality.

Additional editorial support provided by Aline Piva, Research fellow at the Council on Hemispheric Affairs' Brazil Unit, Liliana Muscarella, Research Associate at the Council on Hemispheric Affairs' Brazil Unit

The 2017 General Strike

On April 28, 2017, Brazil saw the largest general strike in Latin America of the 21st Century as 35 million people refused to go to work in protest against President Michel Temer's attempt to set back labor rights by at least 50 years and cripple funding to the labor unions. On the eve and during the aftermath of this historic event, I spoke with one of its organizers, Luiz Gonzaga Gegê da Silva, appearing for the second time in this publication, and with João Feres, a communications professor from *Universidade Estadual do Rio de Janeiro* who is a well known critic of the Brazilian media.

Luiz Gonzaga Gegê da Silva :
The General Strike and the Survival of the Latin American Left

By Brian Mier

Luiz Gonzaga Gegê da Silva is a historic figure on the Brazilian left. Today, at age 67, he lives in a former squat that was converted to social housing in downtown São Paulo, drives a 20 year old car and spends most of his days in the headquarters of the *Movimento de Moradia do Centro de São Paulo* (São Paulo Housing Movement, MMC) working to appropriate the hundreds of vacant tax-scofflaw buildings in the downtown region for conversion to social housing. Gegê is also a member of the national directorate of the CMP, Brazil's third largest urban social movement, with around 200,000 members nationwide. The CMP was a key actor in mobilizing for the April 28 general strike that took place nationwide in protest of President Michel Temer's policies; most notably, his proposal to raise the retirement age as high as 74, depending on years spent in the workforce.

I caught up with Gegê on the afternoon of April 27, the day before the strike, to talk about the current political atmosphere. After the interview, Gegê made me a proposal: Would I like to come with him to shut down a road during the strike? The following morning I met him and a group of 20 MMC members at six a.m. in their headquarters in Sé. All buses, trains, and subways were at a standstill, so we walked through downtown to 23 de Maio Avenue, where we were met by around 100 members of the MST and *Levante Popular da Juventude* (the Youth Uprising Movement). The group walked down a hill and, suddenly, there was a mad race to grab tires and gasoline from a site that was disguised to look like a homeless camp. Mirroring actions that were taking place on hundreds of avenues across the country at that moment, they blocked off one of the city's most important highways with burning tires. For 40 minutes, rush hour traffic was paralyzed, the smoke billowed, and the crowd chanted "Fora Temer" ("Out with Temer"). Then, riot patrol police showed up and opened fire on us with tear gas canisters. As the crowd retreated, regrouped and then started walking and singing through Anhangabau Valley, Gegê said, "Well, this is what we wanted. We wanted confrontation and we got it." That day, 35 million people refused to open their businesses or go to work and transport routes were shut down through all of the major cities across the country.

What is your social housing strategy here in downtown São Paulo?

We have had some great difficulties here in the city center because the unbridled capitalist system always sees the center of the city as a part that should be conserved and cultivated for the powerful, for the bourgeoisie. When we started talking about social housing in the downtown area, many people thought it was absurd that we would want to live downtown. As if poor people and blacks had a location just for them, a ghetto. When I started in this movement, the first thing that I tried to implement was dignified housing in the region. Due to my presence in the MMC the other activists in the downtown area and I deepened this debate. We created a federation called *Unificação das Lutas de Cortiços por Imóveis Dignos nos Centros Urbanos* (Unified struggle of Boarding House Residents for Dignified Housing in Urban Centers/ULC) and we worked to help people know that living in a dignified manner is a human right and a responsibility of the state. Living in a dignified manner is a fundamental right. What good does it do to live under a bridge or viaduct? You do not have your dignity preserved there. When I say that the downtown is a large stage it's because it is a stage that shows the division between the bourgeoisie and the social movements. São Paulo started in this central region and as the city grew this bourgeoisie abandoned downtown to the point that today there are a lot of empty buildings here. Capital is not invested to reform these buildings or to guard them for the future. In other words, the center is a market reserve that capital creates so that a few years from now, the capitalists can sell property at a higher value. But buildings that do not fulfill their [constitutionally mandated] social function should all be occupied by families that do not have any dignified place to live. We in the MCC are occupying various buildings. Two of them were taken from their owners and converted to social housing and in other cases where the city appropriated and converted tax-scofflaw abandoned buildings, we were able to place some of our families there. But our victories are still relatively small because the government still doesn't have this vision that public buildings, or private buildings that are not fulfilling their social function and not paying real estate taxes, should be used by people who already live in the region.

There are people in the anglophone world who say that what happened last year was not a Coup because, at least ostensibly, Dilma Rousseff was thrown out through a legal mechanism. Others argue that even if it was a Coup, Brazilians should no longer worry about that point but try to move forwards. What is the opinion of the CMP on this matter?

There is not a shadow of a doubt that we suffered a Coup in Brazil. And it was not a Coup against Dilma Rousseff. It was not simply a Coup against the PT party. It is a Coup that continues to be implemented on the backs of the working class. The working class is paying a high price for this Coup. And we are still not paying the price for everything they have planned for us. It is going to be a lot worse. It's a Coup, as happened in other countries in Latin America. There was a Coup against Manuel Zelaya in Honduras, there was a Coup in Paraguay. And we had a Coup here in Brazil even though — I said this in a meeting a few days ago and ex-President Lula laughed — it was the crumbs that fell off the table of the bourgeoisie that supported us in the Lula and Dilma governments. Because it was the banks and the bourgeoisie who made great profits during the Lula and Dilma governments. We workers got the minimum possible — *Bolsa Familia* (conditional cash transfer program), *Bolsa Gas* (subsidized cooking gas), *Bolsa Cisterna* (rain water capture systems for families in the semi arid regions) - small things. I started predicting that this Coup was going to happen in 2005 when they tried to impeach Lula. They started building the Coup in 2005 and they continued developing it until 2016. I don't have a shadow of a doubt that if they tried to carry out this Coup against Lula it would have been more difficult for them to pull off. But if they weren't able to pull it off in 2016, maybe it would have happened in 2017. Because the bourgeoisie does not joke around with this type of job. The bourgeoisie is always, in an ever-increasing manner, trying to advance its project to take everything and leave the working class with nothing. They think the only rights for the working class are to have a bitter cup of coffee early in the morning, eat some rice and beans at lunch time and another plate of rice and beans at dinner time – that they do not need meat or milk or vegetables or a good life. Because the moment that the working class begins to have a better life, it will be able to think more clearly. It will begin to perceive that rights are obligations. And this is the issue. But if you see what is happening now, the Coup is an ongoing process. Every day there is a new vote against the working class. The day before yesterday there was a vote in the Labor Commission about labor law reform. They did not allow enough time for society to debate the issue and yesterday it was already voted in a plenary session. 270 Congressmen decided to vote quickly on it so there would be no time for debate. Why did they do this? Because they know that the working class is waking up. And it is waking up in the sense that its leaders and representatives are starting to show them what their rights and responsibilities are. And this is why we are about to start a general strike which will start in great vigor on April 28 in Brazil, when there hasn't been anything like this for many years. On April 28 we may have the largest general strike in the history of Latin America, not just Brazil. The repercussions of this strike could be so big that the other countries in Latin America begin to change their posture. If the strike fails, the bourgeoisie will continue to advance its recapturing of the space that the working class has gained throughout the continent. I am not a political analyst and never went to any fancy university, but I see this with a high degree of clarity: if the Coup consolidates its power in Brazil, the next country where a Coup will take place in Latin America is Venezuela, even though they know that if it happens in Venezuela blood will be spilled. But they are not worried about that. The people who organize the Coup will not die. The people who will die will be their pawns and the working class trying to defend its rights. I lived in Venezuela in 2006 and I participated in a debate and said that a Coup was in the works in Brazil. When I returned from Venezuela later that year, I said this during the opening of the national *Centro Unificado de Trabalhadores* (Unified Workers' Central/CUT) Labor Union Federation congress to a small group of media. In 2009, I was forced to leave Brazil and went to Venezuela; then I returned to Brazil in 2010, 9 days before Dilma Rousseff was elected, and I said it again. When I said this various petit bourgeois intellectuals who were among us laughed at me.

"Listen, cowboy," they said, "you are in Brazil, you are not back in Venezuela. Over there they could have a Coup any minute, but here in Brazil we don't have these kinds of things. We don't have a political climate for that here in Brazil." And now, where are all these intellectuals providing an analysis of their mistakes? Because the left made a mistake in not conducting this analysis. They thought that once they won the election it was over. The bourgeoisie does not joke around.

You fought against the Military Dictatorship (1964-1985) and spent time as a political prisoner in that era. Could you talk a bit about what some of the tactics you used during that time were and what tactics are being used today to fight President Michel Temer and his Coup government?

First of all, the Military Dictatorship never really ended. It just transformed from a green uniform dictatorship to a suit and tie dictatorship. But all of the Military Dictatorship's instruments that we were subjected to during the "years of lead" are still here. It was not taken apart. We never got the right to take down the dossiers they had on our comrades. We still don't know how many thousands of people they were investigating. We should be able to access these records to see how all of the disappearances happened. They found innumerable human remains in the mass grave in Perus (a neighborhood on the periphery of São Paulo) of people who had disappeared. In the bourgeois project, they are the ones who have the power. But they forget that while they have the power, we the proletariat have the force. They may have the economic and financial power but the working class has the force. Unity within the working class is a fundamental tactic - unity between the city and the countryside. When I see a peasant I have to be with him in his defense. Where there is an Indian I have to be together with her in her defense. Where there is a maroon community I have to be there in its defense. I can't be here acting in self-defense when the urban social movements are small, too small to create a mass intervention. Why did the Chinese revolution succeed? Because they achieved unity between the city and the countryside. In the same manner, I say that here in Brazil we need to deepen the debate on unity between the countryside and the city. Groups of social movement members here in the city should return to the countryside and live there for awhile and have new experiences living as peasants. What is the struggle like there in the countryside? And our comrades in the countryside should come to the city to gain experience and knowledge about how to move around in the city. It's not enough to just come here and get on a bus. You have to understand the city as an instrument of defense in the process of class struggle and social transformation.

When Temer took over the presidency, National Public Radio in the United States ran a story which erroneously stated that he never worked for the Military Government, that he had nothing to do with it [Gegê laughs]. So I would like to ask you, do you remember when he was part of the dictatorship government as a public prosecutor?

Temer is a guy who has always been involved with Coups of one sort or another. I don't have all of the details of his career but I know that he was even involved in a Coup within the university student movement during the dictatorship. He has no history of ever being involved in the opposition to the dictatorship. There is no record of him ever contributing to the opposition. There are some people from the PSDB party, for example, who are even today defending the right and the Coup with body and soul, like José Serra, Fernando Henrique Cardoso, and Aloisio Nunes, who spent some time on the side of the left during the dictatorship. They passed through but were not real leftists. Tellingly, when Fernando Henrique Cardoso was elected, he said, "forget about everything I ever wrote. My writings are worthless." Today, José Serra is a guy who defends privatization tooth and nail. Aloisio Nunes defends the far right. But Temer always collaborated with the right. And it was a classic error – I said it at the time and I'll say it again - for Dilma to give this guy the vice presidency. Dilma Rousseff came with all of her baggage as a fighter, as a defender of the working class and here on the other side we had her vice president Michel Temer who always did well during those days. He was never able to get elected to anything - he even committed a Coup within the PMDB party. He used trickery to become a Congressman. He was always at the service of the unbridled capitalist system. And he is one of the architects of the Coup that we are living with today. He played the right cards.

Tomorrow is April 28 and there is going to be a national general strike. What will be the role of the Central de Movimentos Populares in the strike? How many people are you going to put on the streets and where and what are you going to do?

[Laughter] We can't talk about this type of thing. We do not discuss our strategies. I'll just say that all of the social movements and people associated with the *Central de Movimentos Populares* across the country are called to the streets tomorrow so that on April 28, 2017, they can participate in the General Strike of the working class. It can't merely be a strike of the bus drivers and train conductors. It's a strike by the Brazilian people. And we all have a fundamental role in this strike. We are going to be together, organized, taking action and protesting in the streets. Wherever there is a need for a fight, we'll be there. I don't have a shadow of a doubt that if this general strike goes as well as we imagine, we are going to have a change and this change will be, fundamentally, for the survival of the Latin American left. If this strike doesn't work out, the left will be decimated in Latin America. It will start in Brazil and it will go to Venezuela, from Venezuela it will go to Uruguay, and from there it will go to Ecuador. Either this strike is going to work or the Latin American left will be crushed because the right will come at us with all of its rancor. We know that the left isn't so small but it's become a bit complacent. It has to return to the streets. It has to return to the classrooms to dispute with the right-wing youth on a daily basis.

João Feres Junior:
Brazil has Five or Six Fox News Channels

By Brian Mier

On April 28, 2017, hundreds of cities and towns across Brazil ground to a halt as the Western Hemisphere's largest General Strike of the 21st Century paralyzed their transport grids. In São Paulo, the economic heart of the country, 10 train and subway lines were paralyzed and all city bus lines stopped running. Airports were temporarily shut down and nearly all major roads in every big city in the country, including Marginal Tiete, Ancheita and 23 de Maio in São Paulo and the Rio-Niteroi Bridge in Rio de Janeiro, were closed off during the morning rush by groups of protesters burning tires. Most shops and businesses closed for the day, as millions of people refused to go to work.

The strike was organized by *The Frente Brasil Popular* (Brazilian Popular Front) and the *Povo sem Medo* (People without fear) two coalitions of labor union federations, student and professional groups and popular (or poor people's) social movements such as the MST. Organizers estimate that a total of 35 million people participated in the strike.

The strike organizers issued a series of statements explaining why it took place. It was a direct response to Michel Temer's slashing of labor rights and retirement benefits and a rejection of his argument that Brazil doesn't have the money to support the retirement system, especially since it has over $374 billion USD in foreign reserves and hundreds of billions in unpaid taxes by the largest corporations, including R$20 Billion owed by Itau Bank that Michel Temer just absolved.

From the size of the event, one would imagine that it would

have been a major media event. But Globo TV, the nation's largest network, refused to give any advance coverage of the strike. On April 28th, it did not use the word "strike" in its coverage. And coverage of the actual event by all of the major media outlets focused on isolated acts of vandalism over interviews with participants or coverage of what the event was about.

Al Jazeera's May 6 episode of The Listening Post featured a report called Brazil: An Inconvenient Protest for the Media, which focuses on the difference in coverage between the conservative pro-impeachment protests of 2016 and April 28th's general strike. One of the people they interviewed is João Feres Junior, director of the Media and Public Sphere Research Laboratory at Universidade Estadual de Rio de Janeiro. In addition to his work as a university professor and research institute director, Feres is known for his research project, O Manchetometro, which categorizes and quantifies news coverage in the major media on specific issues.

Please summarize the findings of your research into TV and print media coverage of Temer's government. What are your main findings and what conclusions have you drawn about how media presentations influence the debate around Temer and his reforms?

Our research is quantitative. It's plotted in figures so that you can see the exact number of news pieces that are produced and their position regarding a certain subject in terms of negativity or positivity or neutrality. These are the three values. They usually don't do many positive pieces. They are either neutral, describing things, or they make value judgments which are usually negative.

When Dilma Rouseff was is in power coverage was extremely negative. She got three times more negative coverage than neutral during her second term. 300-400 negative articles would appear about her in the major newspapers every month. When Michel Temer took over the negative curve went way down and they started to treat him in a more neutral way.

The intensity of the coverage dropped significantly. He gets around 100 negative articles and another 100 neutral ones per month. It is a little bit more neutral than negative. So the ratio, the difference between the two, is amazing, it's really appalling. And you have to take into consideration that he took office in the middle of the economic crisis and he hasn't solved it. Furthermore his government has been in a political crisis ever since he took office. He had to fire several cabinet ministers because of corruption scandals. So he is not running this great government that would warrant this kind of coverage change.

The media promotes the reforms by using economic language and the language of necessity. I'm talking mainly about newspaper editorials that have more space for reflection and are a bit more sophisticated in their arguments. They say that Temer is not perfect, the way he got in power might not have been ideal but the agenda he's proposing is necessary, therefore, he must be supported. They depoliticize the situation and try to frame it in economic terms to give the whole situation a sense of urgency, of necessity, despite the fact that the merit of these reforms is highly questionable.

What is your overall evaluation of the coverage of last week's strike in the mainstream media?

I think the most striking thing about Brazilian media coverage is that many channels and programs produced a coverage of an event that clearly had two sides to it and only gave voice to one side. It is amazing that many of them still do that - it's current practice. The very basics of professional journalism are blatantly violated. I think that the Brazilian media was very much pro-government in its coverage.

Please describe the difference between the mainstream media attention given to last year's protests that led to the impeachment of President Roussef with the coverage (or lack of it) given to the recent general strike. What is your explanation for this difference?

They strongly supported the demonstrations that led to Dilma Rousseff's impeachment. It was really explicit and it was the exact opposite what they do now. In 2015 and again in 2016, they didn't just announce the demonstrations in advance, they also gave times and locations where the people were supposed to gather. They televised these events 24 hours a day - it was full coverage all the time. They interrupted the regularly scheduled programs with updates about the protests. It was amazing and very intense. *Globo* was the most telling example. In March 2016 there were protests against Dilma and the headline the next day was that the Brazilian people went to the streets to ask for her resignation. Three days later there was a large anti-impeachment protest organized by the left. The headline the next day was that Dilma supporters went to the streets. So the first protest was portrayed as an act of the Brazilian people whereas the latter was 'just Dilma supporters'.

When there were acts of violence in pro-impeachment protests they were described as the consequences of acts of particular individuals who were angered with Dilma Rousseff. But during the general strike, violence and rioting were portrayed as characteristic of the entire situation, the whole protest. So it's quite different.

Given that the general strike had been planned far in advance with major events building up to April 28, how do you interpret the lack of coverage of from mainstream media outlets prior to the strike?

It wasn't only a lack of coverage prior to the strike. It was also the fact that during the strike they acted as if it was just something that was organized by the unions. They implied that only unionized workers stopped and the other workers were stopped against their will. On top of that they associated the strike with violence and rioting. This is a constant framing in the Brazilian media, passing this image that people who go out in the streets to protest are violent and crazy and that they do stupid things. They are not portrayed as people who are lawfully demanding their rights. The media coverage was very negative and they did not publicize much about the organizational work that went on before the event began.

There was little variety in the way the TV news programs covered the strike. Some of the TV channels like *Globo* and *SBT* were totally pro-government. The three main newspapers in Brazil had almost homogeneous coverage of the rioting. They basically characterized the strike as an act by the unions and marked by violence. There is also this interpretation in their editorials that the government reforms are inevitable and Brazil really needs to do them in order to get back on track. The implication was that the strike should not or could not prevail.

Regardless of their coverage the strike seemed to have been quite successful- it spread all over the country and stopped most activities in all of the major Brazilian cities.

Describe how Globo used its media power to actively promote the protests that led to the impeachment of Dilma Rousseff. What does this say about media conglomerates in Brazil and how they are politically aligned?

I like to say that Brazil has five or six Fox News channels. The entire big media acts like Fox News. It's quite amazing. But let me qualify this. They don't present themselves as right wing commentators - they are not openly right wing. They try to pass themselves off as democratic. They try to pass themselves off as balanced commentators who are only saying true and very reasonable things about facts. But they all happen to be on the same side. These companies are very close to each other in terms of politics. They have been conservative for decades and currently they are all in favor of the government. They are in favor of downsizing government programs and are in favor of the reforms. They are opposed to labor rights.

But *Globo* is much larger than anything else on the media landscape. *Folha de São Paulo* has a big newspaper and a big internet news portal but that's about it. *Globo* is dominant. They own newspapers, radios, open access channels, cable channels. They own the internet and cable TV backbones and all the communications infrastructure in Brazil. Their dominance is amazing. And *Globo* was a staunch supporter of the impeachment. You could see that with the coverage given on *Jornal Nacional*, which is the most popular TV news program in Brazil. *Globo* used to be more balanced in its coverage of government. Perhaps it was biased but not extremely biased. It would give some room to different voices from the Brazilian government during PT's terms in office. But starting with Dilma's second term after the 2014 election they changed the way they covered the government and started being almost exclusively negative. It wasn't just on *Jornal Nacional*, but they began attacking PT full time on all of their news programs. Their cable news program was amazing. These guys would run a story on anything related to PT or Dilma or Lula and they would cut to the studio where five commentators would criticize Lula and Dilma. They would talk endlessly about them and always had something negative to say.

What was the primary message that the media propagated during the anti-Dilma Rousseff protests?

During the lead up to Dilma's impeachment there were two sides of Brazilian society. There were street protests for and against the impeachment and they attracted a comparable number of people. But the way they were covered was very unnerving. They would portray the pro-impeachment protestors as representing the Brazilian people and portray the anti-impeachment protesters as being just a bunch of Lula supporters.

The media message was, "We have to get rid of these guys". But when they did it the people who took power were much more corrupt that Dilma Rousseff. So it turns out that the main issue was not corruption but the dismantling of social policies that the PT set up that made a huge difference for many Brazilians.

Is there a segment of Brazilian society that the mainstream media are failing to represent in their coverage of Temer's economic reforms? By downplaying and demonizing the strikers and the anti-Temer movement media, are media outlets catering to a certain class or demographic?

When you see the demographics of the impeachment supporters they were mostly the southeastern white middle class. If you want to give comparative media coverage between the 2016 impeachment protests and the 2017 general strike a class reading, you can say that the media silences the voice of the poor who are the ones that are getting hit the most by the economic crisis and Temer's reform policies. When you cut social policies the worst hit are the ones who need them. The middle class and rich usually need state services much less than the poor.

São Paulo Before and After

São Paulo is the largest city in the southern hemisphere and one of the largest in the World. From 2012-2016 it was governed by a progressive mayor, Fernando Haddad, from the PT party. Although there are many valid criticisms that can be made, including abandoning the housing movements for the first 3 year of his governance, he implemented a series of innovative public policies and reforms. He set up a series of democratically governed, voluntary councils to deepen democracy by increasing public control over his budget. He facilitated the World's largest participatory development plan, through hundreds of neighborhood meetings in which thousands of citizens voted on policy and budget priorities for the next ten years. He was the first mayor to ever tackle São Paulo's notorious traffic problem by implementing policies that favored bicycle and pedestrian traffic and public transportation over the automobile, resulting in a 20% drop in automobile traffic. And he enacted a series of innovative human rights policies, such as hiring a group of homeless people for one year to conduct research on homeless issues. In January, 2017, this all changed. Former Brazilian Trump "Apprentice" franchise star João Doria became the new mayor of São Paulo and immediately began undoing much of the Haddad administration's best policies. He announced that he was going to shut down new express bus corridors, started painting over São Paulo's legendary street art, ordered police to attack groups of homeless drug users, shut down bicycle lanes and increased speed limits on major roads like the Marginal Tiete causing the mortality rate for bicyclists to rise 55% during his first year in office. The following section compares the city before and after the regime change, with Daniel Hunt's interview of Haddad's former Planning Minister Fernando de Mello Franco, and the transcripts of a radio interview about mayor Doria's crackdown on homeless people and street vendors that I gave on the Chicago radio show, *This is Hell* in early 2017.

A conversation with Fernando de Mello Franco, Secretary of Urban Development for São Paulo

By Daniel Hunt

São Paulo is the most populous city in the Americas and with almost 12m inhabitants and over 22m in the Metropolitan area it is also the largest city in the Southern Hemisphere. Far from the collapsing megalopolis sometimes portrayed abroad, it is a city in progress at a crucial moment in its history – thriving culturally and economically whilst indeed simultaneously facing a new set of infrastructure and social problems still unfamiliar to most of its cousins in Europe and North America. A combination of a 500% population increase over 50 years with periods of lack of effective planning and coordination left a series of structural problems for future authorities to solve.

In 2014, under Fernando Haddad, the São Paulo Mayor's Office facilitated the World's largest participatory development plan, through a 9 month process of public hearings and debates in 33 districts across the city, with thousands of participants. In April 2015, I sat down with Fernando Mello de Franco, São Paulo's Secretary of Urban Development, to talk about the planning process and other innovations being implemented by the world's largest progressive city government of its time.

São Paulo's sheer size has to make the planning task equivalent to planning a small country, how did you come to be working on this massive project?

My background is architecture and urbanism. I think I came to this position at a specific moment in this city's history because São Paulo sprang up over a little over 100 years ago through a very deep and fast development process, becoming the biggest industrial city in Latin America. But many things are changing. We are not primarily an industrial metropolis anymore, the economic context has been changed a lot and in the last few years the population growth has neared zero. We have seen a big rise of the lower middle class and so we think that one cycle of the city is coming to a close and a new one is starting. We don't know precisely where or how so this is the moment when decisions will have an impact for decades to come. This is the specific moment where we were legally required to facilitate a new participatory master development plan and we were responsible for driving this process. Everyone knows about the doubts people have about master development plans – is planning so strong that it can really change things? We also have those doubts but at the same time we are totally sure that not having a master plan would be worse than having one. Basically what we have to change and what we are worried about is not renewing or revising the law itself, but that the law at this moment reflects a social pact and that in this we understand that the majority of the population wants to live in a different way. They are totally fed up with the impossibility of living the same way as we've lived during the last century.

We are not talking about laws, we are talking about a shift of culture and this is much more difficult to change than laws. You can write and approve laws but culture is something else.

The debate over the way that the public wants to use the public space is really a symptom of this moment. Part of the population is trying to push us to make moves to reclaim the public domain because one thing is public space and the second thing is the public domain. Public space is a materiality, the public domain is something completely abstract and intangible so when we see the population taking back the use of the streets this is fantastic, although it is also a perversion because some of those movements to take back the public domain are middle to upper class people who also want to privatize it somehow.

So you're concerned about the line between reclaiming the

public domain & gentrification?

Yesterday someone told me a new word that I didn't know. We know about gentrification, but now we have gourmetization, like food trucks – they're very expensive! Of course we have to be aware of those things but we also identify and include new agents the Masterplan which are the collectives. The arts collectives are all over the city and have a huge amount of diversity in their expressions, and I think the grafitti artists, street artists, street musicians and so on are claiming their right to the city and the possibility of having the city, the space of the city, as a form of support for their expressions.

I think this is connected with the social rise of the middle class, because unlike in the past these people are not from the countryside, new entrants, they were born in the city, they already have a culture and I find the possibilities exciting that this will bring in terms of other expressions of urban culture. I think that in the moment we are living now we should somehow strengthen the conditions for these expressions to take place in the city.

I read your article 'Endless City' about this new generation of Paulistanos. My wife's family is a familiar story. They were from the countryside and moved in during the 1980s but she is fiercely Paulistana, she sees all this, the graffitti and so on, as something they've grown up around and are proud of. I find fascinating what you say about this generation who were actually born into these conditions and what they have gone on to create. So, your aim is then, on this side of things at least, to create beneficial conditions so that this culture can thrive and grow?

The thing is that in the political context, what the media wants, and what the political debate always seems to center on is new buildings, new roads, new bridges, and so on.

How difficult does the Mayor's Office find it to communicate positive projects in such a hostile media climate? One example is the cycle lanes. Where I live, in Pinheiros, people are receptive there to these kind of ideas. But just 1 km away in Jardins there is default opposition. Even with this hostility over the past year, at least before the presidential elections, I felt there was progress in winning people over with such initiatives, people who would normally be opposed because of party allegiance. I saw friends, one by one, saying things like "I have to admit, my mother will not like it, but this Mayors Office is doing a good job."

It's so difficult because the debate in Brazil right now is either you are on the right or left but I think that what you just mentioned, the son saying that "my mother has to excuse me but..." I also see that this discussion is not only a social dispute but an age and cultural dispute so we can see young people that belong to the upper middle class and lower middle class thinking alike. They both want bike lanes, they want to use public space. So the battle is tough but I think we need to try to rebuild a social contract by positioning ourselves within the dispute.

But of course, the media has young journalists who come here to talk to us, who smile while they talk and when they go back (laughs) they have to write what the boss, who is much older, wants them to write. We don't know how to cross this obstacle.

The way that it is changing culturally, there's also something in terms of my social group – this move towards reclaiming the public domain is very instinctive. The other side of it is what you described in 'Endless City', which I see here, the idea of these Gated Citadels where you have say, retail, entertainment, apartment blocks and everything is self-contained. This kind of development has obviously been happening in and around São Paulo for a long time, and actually this whole thing about walls and fences in general, the longer I live here, the more I understand this this isn't a recent development.

Yes it is very historical in Brazil.

Some people want these private Gated Citadels and there's the other side who want to actively use public space of the city. Do you see these two opposite visions as able to co-exist?

São Paulo is so big and complex that we can see so many different things coexisting at the same time but concretely speaking, what we want is to decrease inequality. We want to offer more equality in social and spatial terms, which means that we need to create opportunities all over the place and maybe the only way we can find to organize production, organize mobility, organize the environmental challenges and so on, is by redefining the paradigm of transportation.

In the beginning when the British were here building the infrastructure that gave support to industrialization, the railway was the engine of urbanization – it was fantastic. It was a polycentric metropolis, connected around the state, you know the story. But we have to change the current paradigm and changing it means that public transportation has to account for majority of the movement of the city.

But how can I put a rich guy with a poor guy in the subway? Because we don't have this culture of co-existence. That's why when we talk about culture it's a preliminary strategy to create a basis for people to sit together on the same train. Otherwise it will not work of course.

Here in the subway we don't have what Europe had in the past, 1st & 2nd class. We only have one class because there was never any need for more than one class. How can we put all the classes together? There's no other way. We have 4.5 million cars and they occupy a huge amount of space. It is impossible to have two bodies in the same space. It is a physics problem but doing what we're doing concerning this negotiation of the public domain is one strategy for solving practical things such as mobility in town.

When Europeans first come here and they want to go outside the city the first thing they say is 'where do I get the train?' Was there a key moment where the emphasis moved onto the automobile and away from the Railway?

It was after the war. The United Kingdom lost its hegemony and the US came in with the car. This is my theory – I think that São Paulo is very different from Rio de Janeiro. Rio de Janeiro is a very Portuguese city, in its DNA, but São Paulo is British. It's, the railway, the canalization of the rivers, the water production and the energy production. This is the heritage but now we have to think about the future.

I saw a change in planning regulations where now the new tall buildings have to interact with the street. This is another thing that foreigners notice, that there can be nice areas where you can still walk for 3 blocks without seeing a shop, bar, restaurant, cultural space or anything. This is something that seems to be a hindrance to the public domain, as you say.

We passed the master development plan and now we are trying to pass the new zoning law. The zoning law will stipulate how the private sector can build a building but the master development plan can't do that. It is very difficult when you live in a city as big as Sao Paulo. It's impossible to describe a law that says precisely what all the buildings will be about.

We're not talking about what the building will be about but about how the building, how each object will connect with the sidewalk, right?

We're concerned about the ground floor and we're bringing specific rules and many incentives, all these incentives that give bonuses for the builders who open the ground floor, for the ones who put shops and uses that can stimulate pedestrian life in the city.

How is the progress of large projects inherited from previous administrations such as Arco do Futuro *and* Arco Tietê?

That's a good and difficult question. I need 10 days to answer it (laughs). The *Lava Jato* investigation has paralyzed the construction. All of the components are somehow connected to it. The only companies who can execute such a big and complex project like this one are those big contractors who had their operations paralyzed by the investigation, but we aren't giving up.

We don't have a tradition in urbanism in Brazil and we are totally focused on identifying what the critical points of these projects are in terms of regulation, financing and so on, and we're working hard to make it happen. The first step was to reorganize *Arco do Futuro* and *Arco Tietê* in terms of the law and we did it. The zoning law will give us one extra layer and we're working on an infrastructure plan. We are also defining financial tools in order to make this possible in the future. We won't have it in this term, it's impossible in this context, but at least we hope we can leave the tools on the table for the next one.

So from huge projects such as this, on to the cheaper, smaller ones, the urban beaches, the parklets, these new public spaces – these are projects that can have an instant benefit to quality of life. Do you think it is possible that the smaller projects can actually have greater impact than bigger ones?

They have an impact. The municipal government will pay for 32 parklets, 1 in each mayoral district to guarantee it happen outside of the middle class neighborhoods. They have an impact but they're not what we can call structural changes. The structural things demand a huge amount of money. Since this term doesn't have money due to the political and economic context that you know about, this opened a window of possibility to convince the Mayor that even actions that don't cost money can be important and maybe we wouldn't have had space for bike lanes, parklets, etc., if we had the budget for the big projects. It is a very big task, the question is how to multiply them to the size of São Paulo.

Brian Mier:
São Paulo Mayor João Doria and the "Clean City"

For the past five years, I have appeared every few months on the progressive Chicago radio show *This is Hell* as its irregular correspondent for Brazil. In January, 2017, host Chuck Mertz interviewed me about my first impressions of the changes under new "entreprenurial" mayor, millionaire businessman and former reality show star João Doria, from the inappropriately named *Partido da Social Democracia Brasileira* (Brazilian Social Democracy Party/PSDB). Doria's conception of the public domain is radically different from his predecessor, and his first actions as mayor included painting over São Paulo's legendary graffiti art, closing bike lanes and announcing removal of street vendors and homeless people from the city center. The following is an edited version of the interview transcript.

Post-Coup, rightwing Brazil is as violent as post-election, rightwing US of A. Here to tell us about the fallout from the ouster of President Dilma Rousseff, and who may have been behind the Coup in the first place, Brian Mier is our correspondent in São Paulo and an editor at Brazil Wire, as well as a freelance writer and producer.

This week, Brian posted the Brazil Wire *article "The US and Brazil's Coup of 2016." He also has a book that he co-wrote with Cristiano Muller and Karla Moroso, the title of which translates to The Mega Sporting Events in the City of Rio de Janeiro and the Right to the City: an Analysis of the Local Legal Framework.*

Let's start with the story that you sent us from December 29th of last year by architect and urban planner Luciana Itikawa, called "The Golpista Everyman and the Clean City: with far-right attitudes out of the closet, the post-Brexit UK and the post-Trump US both witnessed a surge in hate crime. Post-Coup Brazil is no different."

Here in the United States, CNN reported: "Fears of heightened bigotry and hate crimes have turned into reality for some Americans after Donald Trump's presidential win, and the list of incidents keeps growing. The Southern Poverty Law Center counted 867 cases of hateful harassment or intimidation in the United States in the ten days after the election. The number of reported incidents declined almost every day from November 9th, the day after the election, to November 18th, but the incidents have been widespread, the Southern Poverty Law Center said, and the NYPD reported a huge spike in hate crimes since Trump's election."

What has been the experience of hate crime in Brazil since President Dilma Rousseff was removed from office on August 31st of last year?

I don't have exact numbers on that but there's a feeling that they've been on the increase because just as Trump's election validated all kinds of hate rhetoric in the United States, the removal of the center-left PT government from office has validated all kinds of hate rhetoric in Brazil as well. Homophobia is on the rise. There are now people inside the congressional human rights committee who believe that homosexuality is an illness that can be cured.

The article I posted was about how on the 29th of December, two jiu-jitsu guys were trying to beat up a trans woman in a metro station in São Paulo. A middle-aged street vendor tried to jump in and break it up and he was beaten to death for trying to stop homophobic violence. That's just an example. There are things like that happening all over the country.

What has been the public reaction to this gentleman being killed for trying to protect a trans woman?

I went to the protest honoring the guy and they're trying to name the subway station after him now but a lot of people probably approved of his beating because street vendors and homeless people are not considered fully human by a lot of people in the Brazilian middle class. By conservatives, they're considered to be a kind of eyesore, a kind of garbage that has to be cleaned from the streets.

The metaphor of "cleaning things up" is being used by the new São Paulo mayor (who also was incidentally the star of the Brazilian franchise of Trump's reality show "The Apprentice" here). The first thing he did when he took office was dress up like a street cleaner and appear in public sweeping a broom, saying he was going to "clean up" everything. He's talking about taking all the homeless people and street vendors off of the streets.

What he's talking about, though, is a kind of ethnic cleansing. Because most homeless people and most street vendors are of indigenous or African descent.

Has he said where he wants these people to go? If he's "cleaning" these people off the streets (and that's a horrible, horrible phrase), where are they supposed to go? What is the next stage for their life?

He's one of these Growth Coalition mayors, like the Daley's were in Chicago. It's all about mega construction projects. So he's talking about building a stadium or an enclosed space for all street vendors to gather — which screws up the concept of street vending because street vendors occupy certain niches at certain points in the city where they can sell their products, like the tamale saleswoman in front of the 18th Street El station in Chicago. People going to work want to buy a tamale to eat on the ride downtown. If you pushed her into a big stadium or mall somewhere, people wouldn't drive an hour to eat her tamales.

There's a big music festival they have on the streets every year in São Paulo, and he's talking about moving it into the Formula 1 stadium, two hours by public transportation from downtown. So his idea is just moving everyone off the streets into enclosed spaces, with no real plan about how he's going to do that with homeless people.

Luciana Itikawa writes: "His name was Ruas. Luis Carlos Ruas. He was a street vendor who worked in São Paulo for over 20 years. His nickname was "Indian." Two men cruelly murdered him on Christmas night, 2016. They killed Ruas because he tried to stop violent aggression against a homosexual man and a trans woman. One of the criminals gave his motive (as if homophobia weren't enough): that he was mad at his girlfriend."

Are there people equivocating in their condemnation of this incident? Or even fanning the flames of this kind of hatred? How much anti-homosexual, racist rhetoric is there in Brazilian politics currently? Has it changed since you've been living in Brazil?

First of all, yes, there is equivocation. The police who reported the story said one of the attackers wasn't in his right mind because he had just found out that his girlfriend had cheated on him. So the police were offering semi-apologies for the guy. And I don't understand how they even found this information out because the two attackers are still fugitives of justice. So why did the police bring that up to the media?

More broadly, there's a huge fascist legacy left over from the military dictatorship. A lot of current elected officials, including the President, were government officials during the dictatorship. They got amnesty — unlike other countries (like Argentina, where they arrested a lot of the torturers and murderers from their dictatorship). They granted amnesty to everyone in Brazil and a lot of those people have stayed in office. There has always been a strong far-right in Brazil.

It went a bit under the covers during the thirteen years of PT government. But some very far-right politicians like Jair Bolsonaro began to emerge, and hate-spreading evangelical politicians as well: a congressman named Marcos Feliciano (who is an advocate for the "cure" for homosexuality) ended up, in the last year of Dilma's presidency, as president of the congressional human rights commission. He's gone on record saying that black people are caused by a curse that's mentioned in the Bible. And he's part black. And he's got a lot of followers.

You don't see as much openly racist rhetoric in Brazil as you do in the United States, though. A lot of that is hidden behind class-related code words. Poor people. Northeasterners. Whatever. But they're really talking about black people. The homophobic hate rhetoric and the rhetoric against poor people, though, is as high or higher than it is on the social media in the United States right now. Every time there's some kind of hate crime there are memes that come up on the internet making fun of it, making fun of the victims. I should add, though, that a lot of this social media behavior seems to be coming from places outside of Brazil.

Itikawa also writes in her Brazil Wire *piece: "One of future São Paulo Mayor João Doria's plans is to exclude or expel peddlers and homeless people from the city streets. Doria, who called homeless people 'indigents' during his election campaign, says that he will remove all peddlers from the streets of São Paulo and put them in shopping malls. On December 20th, he said he will 'fully remove' both of these populations from the largest thoroughfares. He also created a controversy when he* announced that he will remove the annual Virada Cultural music festival off of the downtown streets and into the Interlagos Formula 1 arena on the outskirts of the city where, 'it will take place with security, without bothering the population.'"

How much do you fear São Paulo will change under Doria, and is São Paulo a microcosm of what will take place nationally with the new rightwing leadership?

São Paulo has always had a very large rightwing middle class population, unlike other places in Brazil. São Paulo is known for its reactionary rightwing politicians. The governor, Geraldo Alckmin, has connections with Opus Dei, for example. There are a lot of far-right evangelical politicians as well.

And São Paulo is the kind of place that elects former death squad leaders. There are former leaders of the *ROTA*, which is the special forces of the military police from the military dictatorship, who were effectively a legal death squad (and still conduct all kinds of death squad activities). They have an elected state congressman who used to be a *ROTA* commander who brags about having killed 35 people. So in that sense, São Paulo (and the south and southeast of Brazil in general) has always had a more fascist element than the northeast. So São Paulo is not exactly a microcosm of the rest of Brazil.

On the other hand, it's a huge part of Brazil's economy, and the greater metropolitan area contains about ten percent of the country's population. So a rise in the far right here affects the rest of the country. But in general, now, the left has been ostracized. The center-left government imploded and there doesn't seem to be any expectation of a return.

I want to ask you one more thing about the Itikawa article at Brazil Wire. She writes, "If the parliamentary Coup of 2016 will be known as the liberation of all kinds of fascist ghost behavior and all kinds of additional Coups against rights — labor, retirement, etc., — what will be left in 2017? If the rest of the rights and small differences become extinct, the only thing left will be the "Golpista Everyman." The Golpista Everyman is the violent, intolerant, homophobic, misogynist, racist and authoritarian version of that common citizen who seemed to be incubating during 2016 and will gain the majority in 2017."

Do you see the Golpista Everyman every day? Do you interact with people like that?

I kind of try to avoid it. And I live on the periphery of São Paulo, where most people are working class — but I run into them. I have former in-laws who think that way. I see this stuff on Facebook all the time. And some people I've known for years have changed in the last year or two, becoming really reactionary and rightwing in the same way I see with some of my old friends up in Chicago. Itikawa's description of the Golpista Everyman, by the way, sounds a lot like a Trump supporter. I think it's a worldwide phenomenon now, this rise of nationalism, and I don't know what to do about it. Social media is very involved in creating this climate where people have become so reactionary on all sides of the spectrum. It's really a weird time right now.

There's another spot in the article where Itikawa calls individual intolerant behavior a kind of "micro-Coup." I think it's a nice metaphor, and that's why I translated the article. And I do see this kind of behavior, sure. The attitudes have always been there, but it seems like last year's Coup legitimized it so that people feel comfortable talking about it now, whereas in the past they might have kept those feelings to themselves. Now they're spamming it all over the internet and social media in a way that I also feel is similar to what's happening in the United States with Trump's election, and in Britain with the Brexit.

The role of the Brazilian media in the 2016 Coup

In the days after Dilma Rousseff's illegal impeachment in 2016, many members of the Northern media went out of their way to manufacture a consensus, through analysis pieces that were mainly written by their regular foreign correspondents, that Brazil's democratic institutions were working and that what had just happened should not be characterized as a Coup. A common refrain was that it had happened through legal processes. The problem with that argument is that the impeachment itself was not legal. The charges that were used to justify the impeachment were for a budgetary infraction that is commonly committed by all Brazil's presidents, governors and mayors called "fiscal peddling" which involves shuffling budget figures around during an election year to make the economy appear more robust that it really is. According to the Brazilian constitution, it is not an impeachable offense. Furthermore, Rousseff was subsequently exonerated of the charges. In a speech at the corporate front group AS/COA (America's Society/Council of the Americas) a few weeks after the impeachment, Brazilian President Michel Temer explained that Rousseff was removed because she failed to adhere to the PMDB party's Washington Consensus-influenced economic plan, *Bridge to the Future*. Meanwhile, prominent Brazilian leftists announced that a parliamentary/mediatic Coup had taken place, sentiments that were echoed in the most important continental European press organizations, such as *Der Speigel, Le Monde* and *El Pais*. The following interviews, with some of the most critical voices on the Brazilian media, are included in this book to shed light on why so many Brazilians refer to what happened as a mediatic Coup.

Paulo Henrique Amorim:
The Brazilian Media role in the Coup

Paulo Henrique Amorim, 75, is one of the most respected television and print journalists in Brazil. With a career that spans from 1961 to the present, he has covered some of the most important events in Brazil and the World for *Veja* , *Rede Bandeirantes*, *Record* and *Rede Globo*. During the events leading up to his fall out with *Globo* during the 1990s he became a vocal critic of the small number of wealthy families who control the Brazilian media. These criticisms continue to reach large audiences to this day on the pages of *Carta Capital* magazine and on his blog *Conversa Afiada*, which has 520,000 followers on Twitter. Since 2006 he has hosted the weekly news magazine show Domingo Espetacular, currently the second most popular program of its kind in Brazil. He is the author of a new bestseller, *O Quarto Poder* (the Fourth Power) — possibly the best insider analysis of the Brazilian Media ever written. In August, 2016, after Rousseff was illegally removed from office for the non-impeachable offense of "fiscal peddling", Amorim gave a long interview to *Al Jazeera* for an episode of *The Listening Post*. Television interviews are usually long and interesting, but only a few minutes of them ever appear on the final program. We thought it was an important interview to print in its entirety, and *Al Jazeera* producer Paolo Ganino was kind enough to pass his full transcripts to *Brasil Wire*.

"I can fight with the Pope, with the Catholic Church, with PMDB, with anyone, but I will not fight with Doctor Roberto"
How is it possible that during Brazil's democratic transition president-elect Tancredo Neves was willing to face powerful institutions, including the main political party and the Catholic Church, but would not dare to challenge the interests of media mogul Roberto Marinho?

Because he had the right perception which was, and is, that *Globo* is the first and most powerful power in this country. It's more important than the political parties and more important than the church. Currently the Editor in Chief for the evening news at *Globo* is the most powerful politician in this country.

What makes Globo 'Brazil's most powerful company' as The Economist magazine put it?

Because in Brazil, there are no rules for the communications industry. The rules regulating the communication business in Brazil today were written and approved in 1962.

Globo endorsed the military Coup of 1964 and Rede Globo TV started a year after the dictatorship took power. Critics called Globo the "unofficial ministry of propaganda". Does the term still apply, and if so on whose behalf is Globo working?

We are in the jungle and in the jungle the lion rules and owns the game. *Globo* is the second largest commercial TV network in the world, second only to the American ABC. It reaches 98% of the Brazilian territory, it has 124 broadcasters around the country. It's the largest Latin American communication business conglomerate and it has approximately 60% of the advertising business in this country. There is no private television company as powerful as *Globo* in any other democracy around the World.

Globo apologized for backing the military government in 1964. But critics say that the editorial seemed to devote much more space to defending its legacy than to apologizing. Why did Globo feel the need to apologize after five decades? And why was the apology published in print and not aired on TV? The latter reaches a much larger audience.

Globo is the official propaganda ministry of Brazil. *Globo TV* was founded in 1965 and only 49 years later it apologized for supporting, for backing the military dictatorship. And did that only because the Brazilian streets were crowded with youngsters, crying against the government and against *Globo* as well. And afraid of having any retaliation, they said, "Well, we apologize" 49 years later. But actually, in 2013, when the streets were crowded, people went out, *Globo* moved and directed the people in the streets to depose the government. The anchors at *Globo* told the people, "Go this way, and not that way. Go to the Maracanã Stadium, close the bridge..." They directed the masses in the street. Moved by hypocrisy, they were trying to save their own skin. What I can remember about the editorial apologizing for their role in the dictatorship was that it came out as a piece of hypocrisy in the sense that no other company in this country gained more from the military than *Globo*. *Globo* was founded as a front, *Globo TV* was actually a company of the American group Time-life. But the Brazilian constitution said that no foreign company could own a commercial television network. So then the military dictatorship paid *Globo*, paid it's owner Roberto Marinho to buy back the stock that Time Life company had in *Globo*. How they do it? They advertised massively at *Globo*. And so we Brazilian citizens subsidized the owner of *Globo* to buy back the stock that the American Time Life Corporation had in *Globo*. And then *Globo* became the official voice of the dictatorship. The military had to build a telecommunications connection. It was strategic. They had to socially control the country through telecommunications. And they needed something like *Globo* to spread the news, to say everything was going fine. And that's what *Globo* did. In exchange, *Globo* received a license to print money. When I say they have a license to print money I'll give you just a few figures. Last year, 2015, the revenues of *Globo* were around $3.4 billion dollars. Last year the profits were $1 billion dollars which means that he profits are one third of the revenues. That is license to print money. And the profits of *Globo* are roughly equivalent to the revenues of its three largest competitors.

In 1989 Globo heavily edited its presidential debate in favor of conservative candidate Fernando Collor, who went on to defeat Luiz Inacio Lula da Silva before being impeached on charges of corruption.

"Run everything that is good for Collor, everything that is bad for Lula". That was what the owner of the company said to the editors.

The British documentary "Beyond Citizen Kane" focused on Globo's power in Brazil and the 1989 debate. The network first tried to buy the rights to the film. When it failed, the military police confiscated movie posters and copies of the film. Talk to us about this incident and Globo's approach to negative coverage.

Actually, what *Globo* did besides that was try to buy all the copies of the documentary outside of Brazil. At the time I was working with *Globo TV* New York and the President of *Globo International's* New York Company was ordered to buy every available copy of the documentary he could find, wherever it was.

Why did they do this?

Because *Globo* had the control and still has the control over what people say about it. There's a saying in Brazilian politics which goes, "If *Globo's* evening news didn't show it, it didn't happen." That's the policy that still goes on, and that's the policy this interim government is actually trying to follow. And now with the Internet and the social media it's much harder to buy the copies of a documentary. People actually can go to the Internet and go through You Tube and have it. Things have changed, but not much.

Five families own 70% of Brazil's mainstream media. But no other outlet can really compete with the dominance of Globo and the Marinho's in term of ratings and revenue — an estimated 60% of all advertising expenditures in Brazil are spent on Globo television channels. Talk to us about Globo's relation with its competitors.

Globo is like an octopus. *Globo* has eight different companies in all forms of communication, TV, Pay TV, radio, newspapers, magazines and all that. They have interest in real estate and also own record companies. And after *Globo* comes the *Folha de São Paulo*, which is a newspaper and an Internet portal. Then comes the *Estado de São Paulo*, with both a newspaper and Internet portal, and a weekly magazine called *Veja*. But the three others are not as strong as *Globo*. Actually, when you talk of the Brazilian media, you're talking *Globo*. And let me tell you another thing. Sixty percent of the Brazilian government's advertising money goes to *Globo*. Plus, of every dollar invested in advertising in this country, 35 cents go to *Globo*- one single company, one family owned company that is not listed in the stock market. So there is zero transparency.

Globo owns or is affiliated with 340 media outlets. Outside the major urban centers, affiliates usually are owned by politicians or well-connected businessmen. For instance, the families of two former presidents, José Sarney and Fernando Collor, control local Globo affiliates in their home states. How does that affect regional coverage?

There is 100% political manipulation through the local evening news. The owners play the political game through their television systems. And if you have a license to reproduce *Globo* programs in one state you have a license to build different regional stations around the state. And so you control the local politics in the entire state.

I will tell you a story. Right after the military dictatorship, the President was sworn in. The communications minister was a guy who came out of the military. He was the guy who bought all the telephone equipment for the country because the telephone system was a state enterprise. He bought everything he wanted from one company to the other. And then he decided he would never buy equipment from a Japanese company called NEC again. And so the Brazilian operations of the Japanese NEC company went broke. They came to this minister and they said, "What happened?" And he said, "I want your company." So they sold this company to the owner of *TV Globo*. And *Globo* became the owner of a telephone equipment company called NEC. Why? Because *Globo* made a deal with the communications minister. They said, "Give me NEC and I'll give you the power to transmit *Globo* in your state." And this is the guy, Antonio Carlos Magalhaes, who said, "If *Globo*'s evening news doesn't show it, it never happened." Imagine what he did in his home state of Bahia.

The habit of "appointment viewing" has declined worldwide with the rise of on demand video, but Brazilians still tune in devoutly every evening to watch soap operas. And in between telenovelas there's Jornal Nacional, the news show almost every Brazilian watches. Talk to us about the importance of that TV slot and JN's style and output.

The lion's about to die but it's still dangerous. *Globo* averages around 14% in the ratings today. But they lost around 40% of their ratings over the last decade. The evening news lost 50% in the last ten years. The ratings are going down since there is now competition but even so *Globo* and the evening news continue to set the country's political agenda and frame the political discussion. In my blog I say that *Globo* is the lighthouse. Every evening at 8 o'clock the light goes on and shows the way, shows the path to the pirate boats. The boats that will depose Dilma Rousseff. The different boats that were working together to depose a President elected by the Brazilian people with 54 million votes. They didn't know what to do. They were somewhat lost in the high seas. But then, the light came out and they had the route, the way. 'This is how you're going to depose her'. And they did it. As far as the style of the *Jornal Nacional* goes, they tried to copy the American evening news. They built their own system, they built their own benchmarks and their own style but they basically do what the US does - the technology, the way the reporters and anchors work and the stories are edited. So it's very much influenced by the American television system. But it's not exactly like that because there is only one voice that speaks. I'll tell you another story. Ex-president Lula is not allowed to have his own voice on *Jornal Nacional*. When Lula is shown there is the voice-over. There's a voice over his voice, so his voice never comes over the air on *Globo*. If Lula spoke Italian or Swahili, the Brazilian public would never know, except for the official public programs on television that come out every election season according to Brazilian law. Besides that, you cannot hear Lula's voice. He's mute.

In March, Globo suspended its regular programming to cover protests against Dilma's government across the country. Did the network play a role in Dilma's ousting? Please point us to specific examples of coverage

Well, *Globo* did and continues to do that, not only on it's commercial operation, but also at the Pay TV operation. *Globo* has around the clock TV, or the Pay TV, it's called *Globo News*, it's CNN. And it covered the manifestations all the time, non-stop. And sometimes it also did this on the commercial broadcast. But the basic point is that *Globo* has one side, only one side. And TV is still the major way Brazilians learn the news for two basic reasons: the connections for cell phones are still very expensive and the system is not national.

So, a lot of people cannot reach the news coming out of anything except *Globo*. They watch television, they watch *Globo*, because it's their only available source or because they have just seen the soap opera or they're waiting for the next soap opera to begin. That's why we say that *Jornal Nacional* is in the middle of a sandwich - it doesn't have a life of it's own.

João Roberto Marinho wrote in The Guardian that "to blame the press for the current Brazilian political crisis, or to suggest that it serves as an agitator, is to repeat the ancient mistake of blaming the messenger for the message". What's your take on that?

He's a very modest man. He's trying to be humble. He knows he has the strings behind the scenes.

How is Globo covering the continuous scandals in the interim Temer government? Is it giving anti-Temer protests the same prominence it gave to the anti-Dilma ones? Please point us to specific examples of coverage

It's the different between hell and heaven. Whatever Dilma did was hell, was the work of the devil. Now we have a group of saints, working at the Brazilian White house. Actually, they are all suspected of very serious crimes and that includes the entering president. My own blog has denounced and ran a lot of articles showing how he manipulated political expenses without due registry in the Brazilian electoral courts. These contributions were made on the side and he is suspected of using that money for his own party. For these crimes he's been banned from running for public office. He's not allowed to be a candidate any more. And think about that — the interim President of the Republic cannot be a candidate for anything, not even for the city council according to the Brazilian law. And he runs the country. Let me tell you another thing. When the Attorney General concluded that Dilma didn't not commit any crime it was not news on *Journal National* - they didn't show it. So it didn't happen.

After initial hesitations, some foreign media started describing Dilma's impeachment as a Coup. Epoca (the Globo owned current affairs magazine) accused them of being bribed by the left and suggested the foreign press corps should move to Venezuela. What does this say about Globo's positioning in the impeachment debate?

To be fair, that was not *Globo*, it was a columnist of their's and of course it was a joke, it was seen as a joke. But the fact of the matter is, that this interim government cannot leave the country for two basic reasons. One is that many of them can be jailed by Interpol if they step out of the country. And second, they cannot speak by themselves and say it was not a Coup because nobody would believe them. As I say in my blog, they cannot leave the toilet. It's what happened to one their ministers. He got out of the plane at the airport. And when people saw him and started to shout against him he hid himself in the toilet, in the men's room. And I say in my blog, they cannot leave the men's room. I emphasize the men's room because there are no women in their cabinet.

In the past decade, most leftist governments in Latin America have redrawn media rules through controversial reforms — aimed, they say, at breaking monopolies and democratizing the media market. Is there any sign of that happening in Brazil? If not, why not? Has the impeachment been the prize for the PT's inactivity on this front?

Lula and Dilma didn't even try to face *Globo*. They were, and are, afraid of *Globo*. They didn't challenge *Globo*. And that was Lula and Dilma's biggest mistake. They saw it coming but they couldn't react. They gave them money, a lot of money, as I told you. Sixty percent of the federal advertising money, and still, they didn't face it. They built their own demise.

Carlos Latuff Reveals the Tools of Brazil's Oligarchy

Carlos Latuff is one of the World's most famous political cartoonists. Born in Rio de Janeiro in 1968, he published his first political cartoon in a Longshoremen's Union newspaper in 1989 and continues drawing cartoons for unions to this day. As the internet gained force during the 1990s, he began drawing cartoons in solidarity with the Zapatistas, the IRA, Palestinian refugees and other leftist causes around the World. During the Arab spring of 2011, he began publishing daily cartoons on middle eastern politics and developed a worldwide following. In August, 2017, Al Jazeera interviewed Latuff for an episode of the Listening Post called Brazil: Media, Monopolies and Political Manipulation about the media's role in the 2016 Coup. I worked as a producer on the project and they were kind enough to share the entire interview with Brasil Wire. The following is an edited version of those transcripts.

Some people say Brazil is suffering from its worst crisis in decades. How has the media responded to this?

Brazil is going through a crisis but I don't think it's anything new. Brazil's history is full of crises, so I don't think this is the biggest crisis ever. The coverage, from either the mainstream media or independent-alternative would be more accurate – organizations means people learn more about what's happening via social media. The coverage of the crisis by the Brazilian press has been very biased, which doesn't surprise me because there's no such thing as independent journalism. Journalism always takes a side, whether the journalist chooses to admit it or not.

What do you think is the cause of the crisis?

Brazil is an oligarchical country. It's a country controlled by a small number of rich families. In fact, the Brazilian press is controlled by rich families. Brazil's history is full of crises and the current crisis is the result of an internal struggle among sectors of the oligarchy. Dilma's impeachment opened a Pandora's box.

A recent report by Reporters Without Borders calls Brazil the "Country of 30 Berlusconnis". Do you think this is an accurate depiction?

Yes, Brazil is definitely a country full of Berlusconis, right? In my opinion it's a legacy from Portuguese colonialism. There's nothing about colonialism that should be celebrated. The famous Brazilian *jeitinho* came about out of necessity, a way of the Brazilian population resisting the colonialists. Except that later on it became a Brazilian way of life. And we'll take it as far as we can. This *jeitinho* pops up from politics at the very top down to interpersonal relationships on the street. The Brazilian media is controlled by traditional families so it obviously follows the same principles as the old regency. The only reason Temer hasn't fallen yet is because of their internal struggle. *Globo* asked for Temer's head on a plate, that's big stuff. *Globo* helped take down João Goulart and it helped take down Collor. It took down Dilma and asked for Temer's head on a plate. He's only still in government because a sector of the oligarchy, as I mentioned, is keeping Temer there so he can approve the workers' rights and pension reforms quickly. They want this done in a hurry. That means Temer's expiration date is coming up. The press is tied to the banks and the financial markets and it wants these reforms to be approved. If you turn on the TV here practically all of the networks and all of the news anchors support the reforms. The press has a side. The mainstream media's side is money- it's the same side as the financial markets. Since the Brazilian press is controlled by wealthy families, it's also part of the anachronistic oligarchy that still governs Brazil.

Can you talk a bit about your Cartoons?

My cartoons are often used by the leftist press. But nowadays, with the advent of social media, it hasn't only been the left media using them but the average person too, with similar opinions. It is no longer necessarily a union member or a leftist activist. The range of people who access and reproduce my work has really opened up thanks to the Internet. Throughout my career – which began in 1990 right when the press became unionized – the themes have generally been social-political issues: police brutality, state terrorism, corruption, political maneuvers. There a saying amongst cartoonists here in Brazil that goes "there's no such thing as a positive cartoon." There aren't cartoons that support things. The themes are always difficult. And not just in Brazil, the themes I tackle looking abroad include war, armed conflicts and torture. I've also done a lot about the Brazilian military dictatorship. I'm not from that era- I was born in '68. But I've done a lot of work about the dictatorship, about missing persons and human rights violations. I decided to draw this cartoon about the *Partida da Imprensa Golpista* (the Press Coup Party). I didn't actually come up with that term. This term is credited to a journalist named Paulo Henrique Amorim. He's the first person I remember using it. So I drew a pig even though I love pigs. I drew a pig in white-collar and tie, sitting in a tank, alluding to the military Coup. The tank's gun is a rolled-up newspaper coming out of a television. In other words, you've got the printed, written press and the TV. The Brazilian press, more specifically TV Globo, have been responsible for taking down presidents. So that's why I made this drawing, to represent this so-called pro-Coup press party, which is the mainstream media. They have the ability to take down or put presidents in place. This expression, PIG, has long been used by the left and is especially used by PT supporters. But when the PT was in government it could have done more. It could have taken steps to stop this monopoly, to put an end to the media oligarchy that is tied to the wealthiest families in Brazil. Instead of Lula or Dilma's government effectively supporting the alternative leftist press- let's say, for example, *Brazil de Fato* which is a newspaper tied to the MST – they chose to support the pro-Coup press. When the *Folha de São Paulo* celebrated its anniversary Dilma went there to personally congratulate them. She made a speech and hugged Otavinho Frias who owns the newspaper. That's a problem. If you're against the pro-Coup press but also support them it's contradictory, right? I think that during the Lula and Dilma governments it would've been possible to at least start taking some kind of action against the oligarchy that controls communications networks in Brazil. But this didn't happen.

Can you give another example of Brazilian press' influence in politics?

Why is it that *Globo* is interested in retirement pension reforms? Ever since I can remember, even during Fernando Hernique Cardoso's term, *Globo* has always defended these reforms, especially the pension reforms, saying that the pension system was crumbling and that it needs to be reformed. Behind all of this is the banks' interest in selling private retirement plans. So the banks and the TV network are working together. They have a common interest, they have shared interests. That's why you see so many news reports and TV editorials supporting the pension reforms. The bank can't speak for itself; the bank doesn't have a TV channel. You don't see the banker speaking but he has people speaking for him. And that's what TV does. The banker doesn't have to expose himself, he stays behind his desk while the pro-Coup press defends his interests.

Can you explain this cartoon? (See Fig. 1)

This cartoon was made during Dilma Rousseff's impeachment process. It was an irregular procedure disguised in a veneer of legality by way of a procedure that went through Congress. There was an impeachment vote against Dilma. Each congressman openly declared his vote. You saw all of these politicians, infamous hoodlums, saying, "I vote in favor of Dilma's impeachment for my family, for God and for my children." And some of them, most of them in fact, were facing legal processes. They are connected to corruption schemes but were there declaring the most noble reasons to impeach Dilma. The process was utterly embarrassing. That's exactly what the cartoon shows. We showed the World that we truly are a banana republic. I'm in contact with the whole World. I draw about the whole World, about problems from around the World. I understand that corruption is a problem that affects every country and I'll go as far as to say that, from a philosophical point of view, corruption is part of the human condition. I understand that completely. But that impeachment voting scene was embarrassing. I truly felt ashamed of being Brazilian.

Lula was recently convicted of receiving illegal renovations on an apartment that Judge and Prosecutor Sergio Moro was unable to prove he ever owned or set foot in.

Yeah, his indictment. A 9 year sentence from Moro. Well, let's go back to the question of interests. As I mentioned, *Globo* has systematically attacked Lula. If the reason you attack Lula is an issue of corruption, you have to attack everyone. Here in Brazil we have a saying: "You hit Bob, you hit Robert too." In other words if you're talking about corruption, you can't just attack one person. That's the issue. When you present Lula and the PT as the largest representative of corruption in Brazil you're not only sparing all the politicians who face corruption charges today but also a historical legacy of corruption that goes back decades, even centuries. Looking at Judge Sergio Moro's relationship with the press, he's become a kind of poster boy for *Globo*, a hero. You see that in the *Lava Jato* investigation, the huge corruption investigation. If you were to compare US and Brazilian politics, the PSDB would be the Republicans and the PT would be the Democrats, more or less.

So no one, not a single person from the PSDB who's been indicted has been imprisoned. Not one. Even Aécio Neves, who has a dirty record and is among the names listed in the investigation, was set free and returned to the senate. Why is there this distinction? If we are truly talking about a clean-up operation – and I don't think we are – and the end of the corruption in Brazil, why don't they go after everyone? Why don't we go after the Collor government? In fact, Collor was impeached but went back to being senator. The Collor government, the Sarney government – Sarney is still around – and the PSDB government under Fernando Henrique Cardoso. But no, Lula was chosen as the scapegoat for corruption in Brazil. And people bought that. Except that in an unlikely turn of events Temer's rise looks like the people shot themselves in the foot because his government is the worst ever. It's indefensible. His cabinet is practically entirely made up of people facing criminal charges in the courts. There are people with bags of money, videos showing them and audio recordings. Everything's exposed, it's all spewing out for everyone to see. But only some of them are prosecuted, only some are imprisoned. If the aim is arresting people, if it's a "clean hands" operation like *Mani Paluti* in Italy, they have to go after everyone. But they don't. Everything you're seeing is merely a party-politics struggle. That's all. There's no righteous crusade against corruption in Brazil. It's a petty struggle among the Brazilian oligarchies. There's no dismantling of corruption underway. Despite what the media wants to show, it is not happening. Regarding the media do you know a saying, I'm not sure if they have it abroad, that goes, "if you pay the band, you choose the music"? If I'm paying you, you'll investigate what I want you to investigate. Once you start investigating something outside of what I pay you to, you're fired. Take a journalist like Miriam Leitão, for example, from *Globo*, who is very well known. She goes on TV and defends the *Lava Jato* investigation and the pension reforms. If she goes on TV and does this and she's been working at *Globo* for so long, it's because she's towing her boss's line. She's being paid to do this.

If at some point she miraculously sees the light and says something against this editorial line, *Globo*'s ideological or financial line, she'll be fired. That's why I don't talk about independent press - that doesn't exist. No one is independent. We all choose a side. We just need to know if these journalists are on the market's side, with the large companies and their market interests or on the public's side, the public that will suffer because of these labor rights reforms. You have to know what side you're on. You can't be on the fence, there's no way. That theme alone is worth a whole documentary.

You've made cartoons in the past criticizing the evangelical Christian churches. Why are they such a problem in Brazil? (See Fig. 2)

The power of the Evangelical Church, this category called the neo-charismatic movement, has grown a lot, in my opinion, because the utopias of the left vanished with the fall of the Berlin Wall. So today people's notion of a better world is no longer a leftist discourse, it's a messianic discourse. It's not Marx or Che Guevara fighting for a better world, it's Jesus Christ. In the past they had a more nihilistic point of view. They used to say that this world is a mess, the next world will be the best but only if you behave well. These neo-charismatics talk about the next world but say that you can also have a comfortable life in this world. And so you have the theology of prosperity. Why wait to die before going to a better world on the other side? You can have it here. But only, of course, if you accept Jesus as your savior, become part of our church and contribute. Not just with the tithe but also with an offer of love. And so people, despite not having much – and a huge majority of them are the poor – they support the churches and hand them their money. So the churches grew on the back of this promise of a better world in the next life and in this one. The ideology upon which these churches act is a right-wing line. It's conservative, reactionary and homophobic. This is abundantly clear. There's a very famous pastor called Silas

Malafaia who has openly declared his sympathy for the right many times. He's anti-communist. He has strong points of view against homosexuality and gay civil union. It's a conservative and reactionary agenda. There's a presidential candidate from the extreme right here called Jair Bolsonaro who's a former military officer from the Dictatorship years. Bolsonaro has support from this sector. It's no coincidence that Jair Bolsonaro was in Israel recently being baptized in the Jordan River. It's no coincidence that Bolsonaro was at the Hebraica club here in Rio de Janeiro- a very famous Jewish social club- spewing jokes about slaves and black people in front of a predominantly Jewish audience. This religious sector, be it Christian Zionist or Judeo-Zionist, holds the same views as Bolsonaro. And, unfortunately, I can categorically say that Evangelical churches, specifically neo-charismatic churches, are the tip of the iceberg of the extreme, right-wing, reactionary attitudes in Brazil today.

I remember the guy who started Brazilian televangelism- Roberto McAlister. He was a pastor... He wasn't neo-charismatic but he owned the *Relógio* radio station here in Rio de Janeiro. And he understood that it was important to reach people through electronic means. So he included short preaching clips in the radio network's programming. He realized back then – we're talking about the '70s – how important media communication was. This is something that the left should have known. The problem isn't that we have an evangelical TV network, the problem is that we don't have a leftist TV network. We have a network that defends conservative views but we don't have a network to defend progressive, leftist views. So this Roberto McAlister was one of the pioneers. The pastors that came after him understood the importance of the press, the media, to speak to their congregation or potential followers. So they started paying for time-slots on television. That's what Edir Macedo started doing at the *Universal* Church. He started paying for time-slots. And then after he had a lot of money, he thought, "Why am I paying for slots? I'm going to buy a network. I'll have my own network, there won't be a middleman anymore." You can guess what happens next: when you have a TV network, you have the power. Edir Macedo isn't in government but he has the power because he has a TV network. He speaks to millions of people. The moment that he has this access he also becomes a media businessman. He starts to have political power. So whoever is running for election in Brazil has no choice but to ask for Edir Macedo and the other pastors' blessings because they speak to a large segment of the voting population. So everyone goes to kiss Edir Macedo's hand, not just the right-wing parties but the left too. Lula, for example, and Dilma went to the biggest temple in São Paulo with Edir Macedo. Unfortunately that's how it is. These churches' views and standards are archaic to the point of being medieval. They preach things like, "The woman must be subservient to God and the man, the husband" – things that are absurd nowadays. The idea that you would defend such a thing is unthinkable. You have things like abortion and gay civil union. These issues shouldn't even have to be argued about anymore, they should be a given. So that cartoon has to do with the evangelical members of the National Congress. You might think, "Well, the Congress, in theory, should represent the interests of the population." But it represents the interests of groups. Remember what I said about the power of having a TV network? A lot of these pastors were elected because of their popularity on TV, their visibility and their speeches. So all these elected religious pastors organize themselves in caucuses to block progressive laws from being approved in Congress. Today, you have 3 caucuses in the national Congress that they call the BBB: the bible, the bullet and beef. The beef caucus represents agribusiness, the national congress is full of them. The bullet caucus represents the arms industry and defenders of the idea that "A good criminal is a dead criminal". The bible caucus is composed of pastors tied to the Pentecostal churches. They are taking their ancient ideas to the national Congress and they block progressive ideas from going through.

You draw a lot of cartoons in solidarity with social movements like the MST. Would you like to talk about one of them? (See Fig. 3)

This cartoon shows a small farmer from the MST attacked by four powers: the police, agribusiness, the judiciary, and the press. As I said before, Brazil is an oligarchy, it's a country living in a bygone era. But the way in which the oligarchy exerts social control is through these forces. This control has always existed in Brazil. Brazil is not a peaceful country like they want you to think. The problem is not just urban violence. Brazil's history is full of revolutions, insurrections and people's revolts. All of them were crushed by the State. The State is very efficient at repressing, silencing and crushing popular revolts. If you have a country controlled by the regency, it's obvious that at some point you'll have people rising up against it. But what they normally say, despite all the revolts, is that Brazil's independence from Portugal consisted of a man on a horse with a sword. The transition from empire to republic was just a sword in the hand without a shot fired. Slavery was ended with the stroke of a pen. The new state was declared by Getúlio Vargas by tying a horse to the obelisk on Rio Branco Avenue here in downtown Rio de Janeiro. The 1964 Coup took place without a shot fired. So what do we learn from these things? We learn that over here, the establishment, the dominant class, knows when crises will happen. They can't stop a crisis from happening but when it does they act quickly to neutralize it before it erupts because once it does there's no controlling it. They risk losing power. In Brazil, everything is always decided from above. How does the oligarchy control things? With these tools. They passed an anti-terrorism law here in Brazil and it's only a matter of time before they use it to confront the MST and the *Movimento de Trabalhadores Sem Teto* (Homeless Workers Movement/MTST). That's what happens nowadays- we continue to have cyclical crises. Brazil's history is just one crisis after another. Now we have this issue of corruption whistle-blowing. In my opinion, the population is asleep. It's in a coma. They turn on the TV and all they see are scandals but there are no alternatives. The only alternatives they have are even worse. Which tools does the establishment use today to crush popular revolt? They use TV, soap operas and carnival. It's all an attempt to keep you in a coma in front of the TV. If you're not dormant, if you take the red pill, you'll start taking to the streets. And when you take to the streets, the TV no longer has power over you, so it's the turn of the police and the judiciary.

It's just a matter of time in Brazil before they start labeling the social movements as terrorists. They're already rehearsing this. The law was approved during Dilma's government - she was a victim of state terrorism herself but she approved this law so it went through. My cartoons show the tools the oligarchy uses for social control. The first tool is this: religion, entertainment, the soap operas, football and carnival. Think about this: the football hooligans fight to the death in stadiums. They have an anger deep inside them. People have this anger but they don't know how to direct it at the right people so they kill each other. I think that the biggest myth of all is that of the friendly Brazilian, the cordial man, Brazil as a cordial country. When you establish that the average Brazilian is friendly, you then have this argument that there's no racism because everyone is friendly. No one is homophobic, no one is racist. In Brazil everything's too friendly. No one considers themselves racist and you can't confront something you don't actually see. The USA had a policy of apartheid, segregation, whites only. There was nothing like this in Brazil. Maybe we needed signs. You'd have to come out and say it here for people to realize it existed. That's why the dominant class in Brazil is so good at keeping us in these terrible conditions that we live in. That's why they've always been so efficient at silencing dissident voices in Brazil. They mask the truth, they mask the fact that Brazil is a banana republic, a colony, a racist country. But since we don't have "whites only" signs on the bus bench, in the bathrooms – anywhere – we created this myth of the friendly Brazilian. It's all fake. A country that had slavery can't say it's not racist. Even today you can go to certain colonial houses that still have quarters where slaves used to live, torture instruments and slave prison cells. A place with that kind of history can't say it's not racist.

Fig. 1

Fig. 2

Fig. 3

Dr. Ivana Bentes:
The Coup, Phase II

by Brian Mier

Dr. Ivana Bentes is a communications professor and film historian from *Universidade Federal do Rio de Janeiro*. Author of 7 books and dozens of academic articles, she is a long time collaborator with and adviser to *Mídia Ninja*, a nation-wide voluntary collective of young activist journalists that has millions of followers on social media. From January 2016 until Dilma Roussseff's ouster in March, she served as the National Secretary of Citizenship and Cultural Diversity. This interview was conducted in August, 2017.

What is Mídia Ninja?

Mídia Ninja is one of the World's biggest free journalism experiments. It took off during the 2013 public transportation protests, which was an important moment for Brazil. It is a collective, spread across the entire nation, with members living communally, 30 - 40 to a house, creating alternative and new forms of sustainability where nobody has a job and the people dedicate themselves entirely to the group project which is called *Fora do Eixo* (Off the Axis). They are very young people acting in networks within the digital culture who are producing this innovative experience in Brazil and they have nearly 2 million followers on Facebook. They acted as protagonists during the 2013 transportation protests through streaming broadcasts and renewed the language of citizen journalism in an interesting way, which has produced what they call a *Ninja* effect, with thousands of young people throughout the entire nation using their smartphones to express their points of view through an understanding that the media should be activist and should not pretend to be impartial. *Ninja* played a fundamental role in the reaction against the impeachment and is acting as one of the protagonists for resistance on the streets and in the social networks. *Ninja* is aligned with one of the important social movements in Brazil the *Movimento de Trabalhadores Sem Teto* (Homeless Workers Movement/MTST), and is connected with the most important leftist congressmen and women in Brazil from the PT, PSOL and REDES parties. It is a group that is non-partisan or post-partisan or trans-partisan and it's created a team of columnists who come from the most diverse social backgrounds. There is a columnist who is a progressive Evangelical pastor, there is a columnist who is a prostitute who defends sex workers rights, there are columnists who defend GLBT rights, so I understand that it is an important group in Brazil at the moment because it suggests a new form of political movement that is not just based on politics but on the media and on behavior.

The media played an important role during last year's illegal impeachment process against Dilma Rousseff. Now we see that Michel Temer was accused of accepting and paying out millions of dollars in bribes and hush money, based on the solid evidence of audio and video which proves his guilt beyond a shadow of a doubt. But Congress recently rejected attempts to initiate impeachment proceedings against him. How has the media reacted to this and how did its reaction differ from the way it treated Rousseff's impeachment last year?

First of all if you look at the role of the media during the impeachment it is very clear that it was a Judicial/Mediatic Coup. A media group aligned with the financial elites to disqualify the political caste. If you compare the campaign that the media, the judiciary and the financial elites set up for the impeachment to events today it becomes clear that it had nothing to do with corruption and this is absolutely scandalous. It wasn't about political corruption, it was about removing the PT party from power. Because what happened the other day – the victory of Michel Temer who was able to block the investigation against him over clearly proven cases of corruption – made it very clear that we are now in the second moment of this Coup. The first moment was to remove this group from power and this second phase is the consolidation of Congress' management, in close collaboration with the financial sector, of this 1.5 year period before the next presidential elections. This is being done without the people, without democratic representation and apparently with no reaction on the street. Now it is clearer than ever that Dilma was not removed for corruption because Temer is a corrupt president involved in a proven scandal and he will continue in power. The difference from last year's impeachment process is that the campaign against Michel Temer is now being carried out without big protests because there is a deep mistrust among the people that replacing Temer with one of his cronies, Rodrigo Maia, will change anything. So there is a deep disbelief - it is shocking that the streets were empty on the day of the Congressional vote on Temer's corruption charges. People are no longer disputing the presidency – they seem to have lost all belief in the process. So it is a very difficult time. We are stagnating in a swamp where we no longer see the people, revolted, taking to the streets against Michel Temer because it doesn't matter whether he leaves office or not if he would be substituted by Rodrigo Maia, who is also tangled up with corruption allegations from the *Lava Jato* investigation. It is a dramatic moment, this second Coup that we are suffering from in Brazil. And look at this: unlike the unanimous media posture in favor of Dilma's impeachment we actually have a part of the big media turning against Temer. *Globo*, for example, ran a campaign against Temer. But we are at a moment when this political class, that is deeply ingrained in the cronyist system that depends on public money with a purchased Congress, has won the battle against these media forces.

Why do you think the most powerful media conglomerate in the country, Rede Globo, *turned on Temer a few weeks ago, since it was one of the main parties responsible for his rise to the presidency?*

My hypothesis is that they did not believe that Temer had the political power to push through the deep austerity reforms to things like the retirement system. But he just proved otherwise. Now that there was an explosion that proves his explicit relationship with corruption, that proves that he is corrupt, it is scandalous to defend him. At this moment, the polls show that 95% of the Brazilian population is against Temer and wants him gone. There is a strong public opinion against him and it is very difficult, even for a media group as powerful as *Globo*, to sustain a figure like Michel Temer. They had a second possibility for a manager - Rodrigo Maia. I think that for the media groups and judiciary the weaker that the presidency becomes, the better. Because the weaker it is, the easier it is to manipulate and the more it sits in the hands of these power brokers. So Temer is performing the role of manager in the first phase of the Coup but nothing has improved. The economy hasn't improved. It is hard to sustain the idea that he was the solution for the nation's problems. His image is completely exhausted in all ways imaginable. At the same time, he controls power in Congress. He proved that this political caste that is embedded in Congress still has power. He survived this first set of accusations but there are more on the way. There are two more corruption cases building against him. So I think that this campaign for him to leave over ethical questions related to corruption will continue. It seems to me that he cannot be accepted by the media because if they support him now it will become even more obvious that Dilma Rousseff was not removed from power because of corruption. So it seems like the call, "Out Temer" is nearly unanimous in Brazil outside of the Congress, which is fighting for him to stay in power and protect their political appointments independently of popular disapproval. It is a terrible moment. Michel Temer is presenting what could turn out to be Brazilian parlamentarianism. Brazilian parlamentarianism, which would be a political extreme without the people and without democratic representation, is being tested in Brazil. In fact, we are experiencing parlamentarianism right now, under our unelected leader. And even the media is powerless to remove Michel Temer. So it is a confusing and delicate situation.

In your opinion does the Brazilian hegemonic media support the idea of indirect elections next year as opposed to the direct elections we have had since 1989? Do you think they are preparing the public to accept this idea? If so, how?

I think this is exactly what is happening. The campaign that began in *Globo* and other big newspapers against Temer was started by the same people who helped remove Dilma Rousseff from power. They made a bet that politics could be conducted indirectly between the Congress, the media and the judiciary. This arrangement is being tested at the moment in Brazil. It is a new form of Brazilian parlamentarianism which depends on the media and the judiciary, and, without a doubt, they bet everything on the idea that Temer was just an instrument in this transition towards an indirect government. But we are seeing that the political context and the correlation of power between these groups, the media, judiciary and Congress, is more confusing and fragile than we imagined. So in a certain manner I think that the Coup government has been installed in power, but that it has weakened because these groups are fighting among themselves and this is causing the big media groups to flip-flop. *Globo* turned on Temer but *Estado de São Paulo* ran a recent editorial supporting him, saying that it is preferable that Temer continues until the end of his mandate next year so that there isn't any more instability. I don't see that these power players have distinct positions, but they are all disputing with a weakened presidency that is not hostage to these media conglomerates and a judiciary which tries to manipulate these forces as much as possible. But as you said, they are all betting on an indirectly elected government.

Can you give me an example of how Globo is preparing the public to accept the idea of indirect elections?

The discourse is being transmitted through repetition and they relate it to stability, coming out of the crisis, creating a climate for things to get back to normal. The whole argument is built around the idea of instability and rebuilding the economy. This was also the most common justification that Congressmen used the other day when they voted in favor of Temer. They used the most absurd arguments imaginable to vote in favor of Dilma's impeachment: for God, for the family, against corruption. This time around, the Congressmen who supported Temer's continuance in power substituted God and family for economic stability and for the recuperation of the economy. And this is the same argument *Globo* is using to sustain the current economic strategy, either through Temer's illegitimate presidency or through indirect elections. 'Let's continue banishing one segment of the political caste in the name of the economy'. This argument is being used constantly in a very repetitive form on television at the moment, as if there were only one thing important for Brazil. There could be an impeachment, Temer could be substituted for Rodrigo Maia, the legitimacy of Brazilian democracy is unimportant as long as we save the economy and maintain economic stability. It is a fallacy because the country is in terrible shape with skyrocketing unemployment and economic instability that has caused entire states, like Rio de Janeiro, to declare bankruptcy. So once again a fragile, fallacious argument is being built through fear-mongering to maintain this corrupt group in power.

Lula says that over the past year, Globo TV's news show, Jornal Nacional, dedicated 16 hours of negative coverage associating him with reforms of a triplex apartment in Guaruja, owned by OAS construction company, that he never set foot in. In an unusual legal arrangement, judge and prosecutor Sergio Moro ruled his own prosecution successful and condemned Lula to 9.5 years in prison, but there is no credible evidence. It is a much weaker case than, for example, the bank account information, video and audio files that show 2014 presidential candidate and

PSDB party chief Aécio Neves receiving millions of dollars in bribes and threatening to murder a witness. Why did Globo *spend so much time talking about allegations against Lula?*

It hasn't abandoned its campaign against PT and Lula. Even though *Globo* started criticizing Michel Temer due to the corruption scandal, it continues with its demolition project against the PT party and Lula in an attempt to ruin his 2018 presidential candidacy. This process has not eased up. We see it daily, fomented on the social media and the *Jornal Nacional* news program. The fact that *Globo* opted to talk about Temer and corruption at the current moment is because it feels it is a good time to challenge the PMDB and DEM parties who control Congress. But the persecution of Lula continues very strongly in all of the big media companies in Brazil. The campaign to tire out his image continues. The Brazilian media's main goal now is the demonization and disqualification of a leftist political group that is connected to the PT and Lula's leadership.

Djamila Ribeiro:
The fight against racism in Post-Coup Brazil

Djamila Ribeiro, 37, is currently one of the most popular writers and public figures in the Afro-Brazilian woman's rights movement. She was born into a working class family in the gritty port city of Santos to communist parents. Her father was active in the local longshoreman's union and used to take her to the Soviet Union-Brazil cultural center for chess lessons. By the age of 8 she was already winning chess tournaments. She went on to study political philosophy at UNIFESP, one of the best universities in Brazil, and is currently working towards a doctorate. During 2016 she was appointed sub-secretary of Human Rights for the City of São Paulo by Mayor Fernando Haddad (PT) and she currently has a blog following on sites like *Mulheres Negras*, numbering in the hundreds of thousands. She recently wrote the introduction for the Brazilian edition of Angela Davis' seminal work, *Women, Race & Class*. Her new book, *Nos, Madelenas: uma palavra pelo feminismo* (We Magdalenes: a word for feminism) will be released in December 2017 and promises to be a best seller. Since she is an outspoken critic of racism in the Brazilian media, *Al Jazeera* interviewed her for their recent episode of *The Listening Post* entitled *Media, Monopolies and Political Manipulations*. I worked as a producer on that program and *Al Jazeera* was kind enough to provide *Brasil Wire* with the full interview transcripts, which are reproduced in edited form below.

Why do you think that so many people continue to ignore all of the statistical proof of structural racism in Brazil and deny that it's a problem in this country?

For a long time in Brazil we were sold on this idea of the "racial democracy" – that racism only existed in countries that were legally segregated under apartheid like the USA and South Africa, as if we were not living under apartheid in Brazil. When you arrive at the peripheries in Brazil and you look at the people, you will see that the colour of poverty is black. But this narrative was pushed for a long time and the media has played a fundamental role in that – racism is both structural and structuring, it's in all institutional spaces, including the media which for a long time collaborated in creating this discourse. If we look at the mainstream outlets today, including the more progressive ones, there are hardly any black people present in these spaces. If you turn on the TV in Brazil there are hardly any black actors or presenters, hardly any black journalists – this is across all of the channels. We don't get onto the mainstream channels and not just in front of the camera but behind it too. There aren't black directors or screenwriters so there are only a very, very small number of black people in the industry, unfortunately, given the size of the black population in Brazil – and that criticism has to be extended to the progressive outlets in Brazil too because they are also very white and they do not take on the racial debate. For a very long time in Brazil no one has wanted to face this issue, instead saying that we are a mixed country, romanticizing the issue. We're a mixed country but police bullets have a target and they're killing black bodies. The invisibility of black people in spaces of power is glaring, whether that's in academia or political or institutional spaces, so I think it's necessary for Brazil to face the problem that it is an extremely racist country, given that the majority of the population is black and we do not manage to reach the spaces of power in this country.

Can you talk a bit about what has Brazil done, historically, to strengthen institutional racism?

There's was an official whitening policy in Brazil. The initiative that brought European immigrants here during the process of industrialization after the abolition of slavery in 1888 was an official policy. They gave incentives for European immigration here in order to whiten the population because they believed that within 200 years there would be no more blacks in Brazil. So there was, in fact, a policy for this but we are still resisting and we're still here in this country which still denies its African origins and which still runs on the idea that the whiter the better. So there is this ideology in Brazil to whiten the population. This miscegenation, which is so praised with in Brazil and which is sold abroad, is a romantic idea that started off as the systematic rape of enslaved, black women. This continued with the arrival of European immigrants here. So in Brazil this is a very prevalent issue. Afro-Brazilian identity and its roots are not valued and the media has a fundamental role in this because it also follows this ideology up to today – even the fact that we are not seen, or when we are seen it's not the kind of representation we want, it's the kind of representation that is very stereotypical and still. When we discuss, for example, the need for quotas in the media there's a whole furore of accusations that we want to introduce some kind of ideology. "Ah, you're being racist because you are forcing us to hire black people" – we still have these kinds of discussions in Brazil. We have affirmative action in federal universities now and some state level public universities are starting to adhere to racial and class quotas but when we hold these discussions in public or in the media there is always that reaction that tries to invert the logic and accuse us of being racist -all this in a country where we are not represented positively. I think that this has to be understood as violence. I think that invisibility has to be understood as a kind of violence. I grew up as a black child in this country. I used to turn the TV on and I didn't see myself there – in my time the biggest kids' TV presenter was a blonde woman who was assisted by lots of other blonde woman, who was Xuxa. There were 4 generations of *paquitas* as we call them, blonde-haired TV presenters. What did this do to our self-esteem? We turned on the television and we saw that the biggest children's star of the era was blonde and all her assistants were blonde. What is the message that was transmitted to us? That we, as black children, could not be *paquitas*, that the white girls, even if they weren't blonde, could still dye their hair blonde and they could still be *paquitas*. It was transmitted to us, to the black girls, that this space was not for us. And when people talk about this, they don't want to talk about how serious this is, in fact, because this is a kind of violence. The fact is that we do not manage to feel represented and this affects our self-esteem, this affects the subjectivity of black children and the images that are produced by the media, which are extremely powerful, always work to make us invisible or to violate us. The entire time, the message is that this space is not for us.

How has the rise of evangelical churches in Brazil affected the fight against racism and sexism?

The impact is huge because it's in the interest of Evangelical churches to have media outlets in order to indoctrinate, in order to have access to a hugely important space to reproduce their discourse, beliefs and ideology. The problem is that this coincides with the emergence in politics of the evangelical caucus. I'm not talking about the faith of individual people but about institutions and what they represent, particularly here with many politicians. In terms of woman's rights they oppose the decriminalization of abortion, which was a very important step for women, and *Record* specifically has been very counter-productive in the way it has criminalised Afro-Brazilian religions like *Candomblé*. Indeed some groups recently sued *Record TV* in the courts over this issue, for demonizing Afro-Brazilian religions, portraying them as devil-worship even though this concept doesn't even exist in Afro-Brazilian religions and some groups won their cases. *Record* was then made to broadcast programs which spoke respectfully about these religions. So I think the power that a church ends up having in Brazil is worrying, the number of neo-pentecostal churches has grown enormously in Brazil and it's not just the case of *Record*, which is owned by the leader of the Universal Kingdom of God Church, but there are other channels where other churches purchase programming hours- big broadcasters with large audiences here in Brazil- and we see the number of followers rising and the discourse which is propagated by many of these religious leaders is very much against Afro-identities and against woman's rights. We have a very important debate at the moment in Brazil which was created by the conservative right, called "schools without political parties", which proposes, for example, not discussing subjects relating to gender or sexuality in schools. So in São Paulo for example, during voting for the Municipal Educational Plan, the issue of whether or not to include gender on the curriculum almost provoked a war, especially among people linked to the neo-pentecostal churches. So it wasn't included. They said it would encourage people to become gay. They created an interesting term, "gender ideology" saying that we wanted to "create a gender ideology", when in fact a gender ideology already exists in Brazil. We simply wanted these issues to be studied in Brazilian schools as a way of battling this very gender ideology that allows a woman to be sexually assaulted every 5 minutes, and for a woman to be raped every 11 minutes. So we understand that these Evangelical churches are not acquiring space on television by accident – it's precisely to keep their ideologies visible and to make it impossible for us to advance, especially regarding some very important issues, and in a country that is politically secular – theoretically, at least – although we see this kind of discourse spreading more and more in Brazil.

The biggest Brazilian media companies remain in the hands of a few, wealthy families. Why?

I don't think the Brazilian media does a good job of informing its public, which goes back to the fact that we haven't undergone a process of democratization of the media in Brazil. We've ended up with a monopoly concentrated in a few hands.

And they are people whose objective is in fact to maintain the status quo, to maintain a dominant ideology. We have very little discussion in the mainstream media that strays from the hegemonic ideology. We have very few black people on the media – this in Brazil where the majority of the population is black. If you turn the television on in Brazil for example you would think that you were in a Northern country, not in Brazil. We aren't well informed because of this monopoly, because of this monopoly of power which even the recent leftist governments didn't tackle, i.e. the democratization of the media in Brazil.

It's a system of electronic strong men. If we look at the TV, even though they are public concessions in Brazil, or at the printed newspapers, it's all the same groups producing this media. Even online we are under the illusion that we have a wider choice. I mean, of course we do in as much as it gives us the power to create our own sites or blogs, but even those big media groups are online with their websites which get millions of hits. So all of these spaces, unfortunately, maintain the dominant narrative that has been transmitted throughout Brazil since the impeachment of President Dilma – which we understand as having been, in fact, orchestrated by them. It was a Coup in fact, as we say, a media Coup demonstrating the power that the media has to criminalize certain political parties, to maintain the dominant narrative, and contributing to the situation in which we find ourselves today in Brazil.

What we mean when we talk about these strong men is a situation found especially in the Northeast of the country, where power is concentrated in the hands of very few people called *coroneis*, who dictate the rules within these places. Even today in Brazil there are still people like this all over the country, who have veritable dictatorships in some cities and states, who maintain power and dictate what must be done and how. So what we experience today in Brazil with these media *coroneis* is that they produce the discourse and we don't have a way of contesting it. We end up having no way of fighting it because we don't have access to those spaces, even though today in Brazil we're in an interesting moment in terms of activism as the internet provides an interesting space. Next to the dominant narrative we can't create an effective counter-discourse because the dominant media outlets are in the hands of these *coroneis*.

Why, during 13 years of center-left PT Party government, were they unable to regulate the Brazilian media?

When the possibility of regulation was raised in Brazil a few years ago, what was the reaction from these mainstream media groups? That this was tantamount to censorship, that this is what happens with regulation in other countries. They used the example of Argentina and they sold the idea that the government wanted to censor the media. The lack of regulation, the lack of the democratization of the media in Brazil, means that these groups still have the power, still dominate the discourse and influence the population in accordance with what they want. It's extremely worrying that in Brazil we still don't have media regulation and that we haven't been able to tackle this issue head-on. In some countries you have one channel that offers one version of the discourse, and another that contests it somehow but here in Brazil we don't have this – this doesn't exist on terrestrial mainstream TV here. It's very damaging because the power of these mainstream media outlets remain in the hands of a few people and we don't have a way of countering that discourse, of offering a counter-hegemonic discourse, of showing the other side of the story. So what we're left with in Brazil is this hegemonic discourse which sometimes is highly hypocritical and misleading because they spend two hours offering one side of the debate and then question just one person on the other side. Then they say "no, but we show the other side too" – but what's the editorial line they're transmitting, what's their vision? We know what it is. It is to reproduce this exclusive discourse, to reproduce the dominant logic of those who are in power. So the fact that there's no regulation means that we're at the mercy of these groups.

How does this affect coverage of the majority Afro-Brazilian population?

First of all we have very few spaces in which to have these debates, where the media could be informing the public, so when we have debates about affirmative action in Brazil, when we discuss the genocide of the black population in Brazil and the fact that every 23 minutes a young black person is assassinated, what's the narrative that gets shown? It's always: "confrontations in the peripheries and criminals were murdered" – so there isn't a narrative that serves even to inform the Brazilian public. Brazil was the last country in the World to abolish slavery, an extremely violent country in which affirmative actions, which although they had been discussed historically within the black movement for a long time, were only adopted in recent years. For example, when it's a black man it's a criminal, or a drug-dealer but if it's a white middle-class guy he's portrayed as a young man caught with drugs on him. There's always this narrative which criminalises the black population, and when we talk in terms of institutional policies we cannot forget the role of the media in the extremely worrying political process that Brazil is living through at the moment. When we say there was a media Coup it's because there were hours and hours of criminalisation of certain political parties in Brazil, a narrative that it was necessary to implement order in Brazil and when you went down to the streets you saw people reproducing these ideas. They don't even recognise that, independent of the mistakes made by the recent governments in Brazil, the narrative that was sold was that they were a criminal organisation as if these parties invented political corruption, as if it wasn't systemic. So the whole narrative sold around what has happened in Brazil, which we see even the poor reproducing, was built by the media. The power that this media has is fundamental to the crisis that Brazil is experiencing today, in transmitting this vision – at no point was there a space to say what was really happening, where we were seeing judges becoming hero superstars, the partisanship of the judiciary in Brazil, and the creation of certain figures as saviors which, unfortunately has been sold to the Brazilian public. So we didn't have any way of countering this because the media is in the hands, unfortunately, of these *coroneis* who are going to reproduce this kind of discourse.

Brazil's most popular TV shows are the soap operas, the telenovelas. How do they influence the county's racial dynamic?

Of course, entertainment is in some ways different from the news, but it also communicates in a way that is discriminatory, firstly when we are not seen, secondly when we are there, the black woman is extremely objectified and ultra-sexualised. The only spaces that we have in the media are either when we are sub-altern or when our bodies are being exotified. In recent years this has been changing, very much because of the pressure coming from social movements. Today there are some channels in Brazil that seek us out, that want to hear our opinions about some issues but not because, in my view, they understand the issue. For example, a mini-series came out a few years ago in which the four stars were black women, so they said 'look, it's the first time there are four black women protagonists'. But the characters they put out there were very stereotypical so we made a lot of noise about it online and the series only lasted one season before it was taken off the air. Today, because of the Internet, we are able to make some noise about this and sometimes we even manage to reach the mainstream media in some regards. It's not actually the case that they get it but more that we manage to bother them when we see certain representations which only serve to legitimize the place that they have created for us. There is a Brazilian filmmaker called Geralzito who recently made a documentary about the *telenovelas* in Brazil and it's extremely absurd the way they whiten the characters. In series adapted from books in which the main characters are black, for example, when they make it into a *novela* they make the characters white. When the directors are asked about it they just say 'oh, we didn't think about that'. And when we question why they put a white actress in the role of a black character they say 'it doesn't make a difference'. So, whenever we discuss this it's as if black people aren't human – they don't recognise our humanity. This happened in very famous series in Brazil in the past, for example *A Escrava Isaura*, and *Chiquinha Gonzaga*, where black women characters where played by white actresses. Today this perhaps wouldn't happen, not because there's been a change in conscience but because we have a platform where we are able to protest and manifest our indignation.

Can you talk a bit more about the series that you helped take off the air?

The series was called *Sexo e as Nega* (Sex and the Black Girls). In fact, according to the director, the idea was to reproduce *Sex and the City* but that show is American and it's about four successful white women and here in Brazil it was going to be about four black women from the periphery. The periphery here is not the issue but there would be scenes like, for example, a security guard looks at a woman in a shop and then it goes to the next scene and they are having sex in a car. Its black women portrayed as if that's all that black women do in this country, as if we don't study, don't work, and don't have any kind of life beyond this. It was a series that was only on the air for a short time because we made a lot of noise about it. We protested a lot against it because we are tired of black women being represented exclusively in this kind of exotified, sexualised way, as if we could not also be firefighters of teachers or anything else. So the issue for us was not being placed in the periphery because most of us are in the peripheries because we live in a country that is extremely racist.

The issue wasn't that. The problem was representing us without bothering to represent all of our human complexities. We don't have any problem at all with our own sensuality which is one of the counter arguments used against us, by which they want to portray us as being self-righteous about it. The problem for us is not the sensuality, the problem for us is believing that this is the only possible trajectory for us, as if we couldn't be anything else. It's very violent to show images like these, especially for black girls to watch, that show their bodies as simply a receptacle implying that we're a mere instrument for the men's pleasure who are not able to control themselves. That's still the image of black women that is transmitted in Brazil and this series reinforced that role further. That's why we put ourselves against it and at the time it was the same old story with the series creator acting really offended, saying, 'but I put four black women in the lead roles', as if he was doing a favour for us. TV as a public concession does nothing more than the bare minimum when it comes to employing black people. There are still hardly any in Brazil but they often come at us as if we should be grateful for them for employing a few black women. Our issue goes beyond being represented, our issue is how we are being represented.

Escrava Isaura (Isaura the Slave) is a classic in Brazil. It tells the story of an enslaved woman who is the daughter of a white man and a black woman, and this was made into a *novela*. There have been various televised versions of this in Brazil, on different channels. It was on *Globo* first and then on *Record*, but on both channels it starred a white women playing the lead role. In the book she is the daughter of black and white parents but in the mini-series and *novelas* she's played by white actresses, Lucelia Santos and Bianca Renaldi. *Chiquinha Gonzaga* was a popular miniseries about a very famous black classical musician and composer in Brazil but when it came to telling her story she was represented by the white actress Regina Duarte. This is an example of the whitewashing of our history. When they tell the story – because they can't avoid telling it, it's so famous – when it comes to representing it visually, it's white women who are there taking up these spaces. As if it wasn't enough, Machado de Assis, the most famous Brazilian novelist, was black but there was an advert once that portrayed him as a white man - a commercial for a public bank. In order to say that he wasn't black they say 'he wasn't black he was mulatto'. So there are always these attempts to whiten these great historical figures and they make it hard to even recognise our own history. We have an education system in Brazil that is legally obligated as of 2003 to include African and Afro-Brazilian studies in the curriculum, but unfortunately there are no punishments for non-compliance associated with it. So if schools do not follow it and if there's no political will in certain cities they simply don't do it. So what we have is this white history, a history told from a euro-centric point of view, and the media simply follows this euro-centric reproduction as if black people had not in fact contributed to the building of Brazil. So when we are represented it's always in this stereotypical place, the black man is always a criminal, a drunkard, the vagrant, and the black woman is always either subaltern or exotified, with extremely rare exceptions. And when we are to be found in these spaces it's one among thousands. There was a film recently in Brazil which was very successful and got great reviews, called What Time Will She Be Back? It is about a maid and the relationships in her workplace. The actress chosen to play the part is an actress who's not white, we would say she is of indigenous ancestry, but the daughter was played by a white girl. So it's always this issue, when we criticise the novelas to say that they only put black actors in the roles of maids, what's the reply of many directors? That 'we're just reflecting the reality' – right? Lots of black women are maids, we are just reflecting the reality. And they are characters who have no on-screen family life. It's as if they're just floating there in the *novela*. They appear from time to time- always infantilised- and they have no family and no other life. And when it came to portraying this life at the centre of a film, in a film that was hugely successful in Brazil, what did they do? They put a white woman in the role, not a black woman. So the question I ask is, why didn't they put a black woman in the lead role, seeing as you're always saying that you're only portraying the reality of Brazil? And the reply was that there are also maids who are white. So is seems our situation is this, that we are always at an impasse. It's a tautology - when it's a case of not having any black characters at all, OK, but when it's about the way they are represented… ah, then… The question that I ask is how can we talk about domestic work in Brazil without talking about racism? About the direct relationship between slavery and domestic labour? So at the point when the issue is addressed, and gets brought before a wider audience, we're not even there – even when we are talking about a reality that is true for millions of black women all over Brazil.

What can be done to push for media regularization in Brazil?

I think that social movements really need to take this issue of regulation on in Brazil. I think it's a debate that is really relevant to us. it's an issue that is progressive but still white-dominated. I think that the movements for woman's rights, for example, need to understand that this is a common struggle also, but this is a discussion that needs to make the public aware of the need for regulation in terms both of property and in terms of the content that is broadcast, because we cannot continue to accept all of these media outlets being in the hands of so few. What is even more troubling is that they are public concessions but they do not fulfill their public mandate in Brazil- to the contrary. Who knows what the next year will be like in Brazil. It's going to be an election year and we're living a difficult moment. But I think it's a struggle we need to think of as essential if we really want to produce counter-narratives and counter-hegemonic discourses and I think that the black movements need to understand this issue, because we can't talk about democratization in Brazil without talking about the progression of the black population in Brazil and without the black population participating from within these spaces.

What kind of advances have been made in the fight against racism?

In recent years there have been some small advances, mostly because of the black woman's movement in Brazil. The black woman's movement has grown a lot. *Geledes*, in Salvador, is now the biggest social movement in Brazil because we go straight to the point. We understand there is a space for us on the internet despite all of its limitations in Brazil which is an enormous country in which not everyone has access to it. There are filmmakers, sites, blogs and activists like me that have gained a lot of visibility because of the internet. So it's an interesting space for knowledge production and for information to circulate. In the last few years we managed to raise some issues in the media because if things aren't the way we want them to be, we go after the issue. For example, two years ago a big institution here in Brazil commissioned a theatre play in which the actors were in black-face – this was in 2015. A huge movement against it started growing online and these activists created a debate about black-face and it was understood that no matter how much the actors wept about it, it was unacceptable and that the play could only go ahead without the black-face. Then this institution talked to the activists, created a discussion group, hired people to talk to them, and today they are doing some really interesting work in terms of giving visibility to black artists and writers. That's one example of an action that began on the internet. Another example is that today you have mainstream TV channels holding discussions about race and gender and hiring some people as consultants for some productions. There've been some programmes about racism and feminism on TV because of the pressure we've created online. Today, for example, there's going to be a whole programme about racism but it will only go on air at midnight. So although we have made some progress and it is no longer possible for them to ignore certain issues, it's still not on at 8pm, it's not a major story on the TV news about racism in Brazil. I consider these to be small steps but they are small steps that were made because of the pressure we're creating and not because of a change of awareness or because people have thought, themselves, about the need to discuss this or to have black people in these spaces. But what's interesting is the number of media collectives that have emerged in the peripheries. It is fantastic to see people creating media collectives in various periphery neighborhoods in Brazil to inform their own communities and creating discussion forums and I think that we need to transcend these tools like Facebook and create new ones. But anyway, we are starting to see more activism from groups who are still ignored but who are raising their issues, so the number of periphery media and journalism collectives has grown a lot. But I think that we activists, especially feminist activists, have understood the internet as a space, even though many prominent left-wing intellectuals are ridiculously reluctant to use the internet. We're still often viewed as people who just want to be seen - that's what they say. Our response is yeah, we do want to be seen – that's exactly what we want. Because we're tired of being invisible, and we want to raise our issues but we want to do that in the first person. We're tired of being objects and having no right to reply.

The Future

Most of the interviews for this book were conducted between late 2014 and mid 2017 and their questions were formulated to learn what key figures in the Brazilian left thought about what had really happened during the process that removed Dilma Rousseff from office and what its repercussions were. There was consent that this impeachment process was, indeed, a Coup. As I began compiling the interviews, another question entered my mind. Now that the Coup has taken place and a corrupt rentier class had taken over the country and was rolling back the social welfare state, what could we do about it? The following three interviews were conducted specifically for this book, during December 2017. In each case, I asked the interviewees about the current context and how we arrived here, what they think will happen during the election year of 2018, and how the left can regroup after this staggering blow, how the left can take back power and undo the damage that has been done to the Brazilian people. The following block of interviews includes a national social movement leader, an NGO manager with a long history of work on poverty alleviation projects in the Brazilian northeast and a short interview with busy 36 year old presidential candidate Manuela D'Avila.

Miguel Lobato:
Inside the MNLM Squatter's Movement

By Brian Mier

When the Brazilian Military Dictatorship ended in 1985, activists began a nationwide campaign to petition for people's amendments to the new constitution, which was ratified in 1988. One of the most important victories was ratification of people's amendments 182 and 183, which guarantee the right for anyone who doesn't own property to squat on land that is not being used productively and is not part of an environmental protection area. It also gives landless citizens the right to squat in any abandoned building in which the owner owes back taxes. In both cases, due to laws that were subsequently ratified to enforce the amendments, the responsibility falls on the government to remove the land from its owners, pass the deeds to the squatters and provide funding to upgrade the living conditions and utilities delivery to meet basic standards of what is defined as dignified housing. Since 1988 when the constitution was ratified, more than half a million Brazilian families have received land deeds after squatting in informal settlements and empty buildings. Miguel Lobato, 50, is one of the leaders of the *Movimento Nacional de Luta pela Moradia* (National Housing Struggle Movement/ MNLM) a poor people's or "popular" urban social movement that fights for squatters' rights in 26 Brazilian states. He is also a member of the *Fórum Nacional de Reforma Urbana* (National Urban Reform Forum/FNRU) directorate. I met with him on December 9, 2017, while he was in São Paulo for a meeting of the *Frente Brasil Popular*, the broad based coalition that was organized in 2016 to fight against the Coup.

What is the MNLM?

The MNLM started during a nation-wide mobilization that took place in Brazil in 1987. We were working to create a people's amendment for urban reform to the new 1988 Federal Constitution. We spent 1987 and 1988 debating the Federal Constitution in communities across the country and we managed to help approve articles 182 and 183, which declare adequate housing as a basic human right and require the government to prioritize the social right to property over the profit motive. During the mobilization for the people's amendments, we created a national, poor people's social movement for housing.

What does the MNLM do?

We fight for urban reform. Housing is our main priority but we also fight for the right to the city, for sanitation, water and sewage collection and treatment, for urban mobility, and for the legalization of informal settlements.

What are the strategies that you use in this fight for housing rights?

We have several different strategies. Our main strategy to guarantee that adequate housing policies are implemented in our country, in accordance with our constitution, is to coordinate occupations of vacant urban land and empty buildings. Through these efforts, some 50,000 of our working class members have gotten the deeds to urban land and apartments in 26 states in Brazil.

You are from Belém, one of the Brazilian cities that has the strongest social movement traditions. Can you talk a bit about the housing issue there?

Housing in the Amazon region is complicated. Para is a rich state full of very poor people. There is a huge housing deficit, both in absolute numbers and from a quality standpoint. Most of the urban population of Para live in informal housing, without the legal titles for their land. Many of them live in wooden stilt houses on the edges of rivers, inlets, canals and streams in medium and large cities, or they live very far from the urban centers. Belém, the capital of Para, is a city that is completely made up of squatters' occupations, crisscrossed with canals, rivers and streams that feed into the Amazon River. Only 4% of the city is connected to the sewage grid. All of the hydro-graphic basins are occupied with wooden stilt houses. Our social movement was born in the squatters' occupations. It is a big challenge to fight for adequate housing rights in Para. Our society is very capitalist, so the rich exert an intense level of violence against community leaders and occupations. We managed to pressure the state to implement a basic housing policy after a lot of struggle, but it's a violent state and when they order forced mass evictions it's very violent and the squatters leaders are persecuted. They are still killing social movement leaders in the countryside and the cities of Para.

How did you get started in the housing rights movement?

Let me start by saying that nobody from the working class in this country ever achieved anything without fighting for it. Everything that the Brazilian population achieved happened through a lot of fight. Only people who have lived under the black plastic tarp know how hard it is to live in a squatters' occupation. 70% of the Brazilian population have lived on occupied land at one point or another in their lives. The Brazilian housing policy only exists on paper.

I've fought for housing rights since I was 7 years old. I was born in a neighborhood that had been completely occupied. We kids played soccer in the middle of the dirt street, in a neighborhood that had no sewage collection or treatment, no sports, culture and leisure options, where the state was totally absent. A local businessman sent thugs into our neighborhood to start knocking down houses. A man came up to our neighbor's wooden shack with a chainsaw and my little friends and me sent him running under a shower of rocks. The businessmen who were trying to coordinate a mass eviction and land grab called us in to ask why we were throwing rocks at those people. From that day forward I've never left the housing movement. I entered the movement and didn't even know I was in it. We started fighting for housing rights in the 70s and through the 80s and 90s it was very difficult due to police repression.

Some middle class conservatives like to try to discredit social movements like the MNLM by saying that they are a group of people who suck up to the PT party, that they are lazy, don't work and just want free handouts from the government. How would you respond to this and what is the MNLM's relationship with the PT party?

It is true that there are a lot of people who support the PT party in the MNLM, but we have members who support all the different parties and we have members who don't like any political party at all. Our task is to organize people who need housing and who need the right to the city. We fight for democracy. We think that the Lula government got a lot of things right, but they made a lot of mistakes too. For example during the transition from Lula to Dilma's government they stopped funding the PAC Favela Urbanization project. This was a mistake because this program solved the problems for the population that was living in shacks, in stilt houses over the mud, who lived in occupations that were thirty years old but still didn't have any infrastructure, running water, paved roads or schools. I live in a community that benefited from this program. It improved the quality of life for the 3000 families that live in my neighborhood on the periphery of Belem. It was a mistake to stop the program.

The Lula government made a lot of mistakes, but despite that it still did more for the poor than any other government. When they made mistakes we protested against them. We took to the streets to dispute Lula and Dilma's urban policy. But despite whatever mistakes they made, we are against last year's Coup, against the phony impeachment and we continue to oppose the Coup government. Refusing to recognize Michel Temer's Coup government doesn't mean you are a PT supporter. We oppose it because we defend democracy. We knew that what was really being organized was a criminal gang. It's an organized crime group that no longer hides its ideas from the population. Its *modus operandi* is to act as an organized crime group inside the Brazilian Congress. If they tried to honestly present their platform of privatizations, destroying the retirement system, ending labor rights and bringing Brazil back to slavery days, they would never win a single election. They were only able to push through their agenda through a Coup. The military didn't want another dictatorship like in 1964, so this Coup was pushed through by the parliament and the judiciary and they put the puppet Michel Temer in charge to serve their interests by dismantling the country. Within this context, the working class had to be united. What is the way out? It's through the leftist political parties. We don't agree with the people who characterize our movement as being part of the PT party. I wish the PT party would give us money. We never took one cent from them.

We think that the PT party still has a viable program that is focused on the low income sectors of the population. We think that it is a party that was created from the bottom up, through dialogue with society. This is why we support the left. We are a social movement that defends the idea of socialism. We believe we will only solve the problems of the Brazilian people with socialism. Our organic militants know this. We don't fool ourselves with this or that government program. We believe the government needs integrated policies that prioritize the poor. The poor population has to study a lot so that it can understand what a socialist society is and choose it. We are against the idea of creating socialism by decree, from the top down. You can't just have someone come up and say "now

Brazil is a socialist republic", overnight. This doesn't work. This isn't what socialism is supposed to be and it won't work out if it's done this way. Socialism requires a change of thinking. We have a lot of organizing work to do for the people to defend socialism.

In Argentina, a conservative judiciary under a neoliberal president is trying to arrest Kristina Kirchner before she can run for the senate. Here in Brazil a conservative judiciary is trying to arrest Lula so that he can't run for president. Do you think that Lula will be able to run for office? If he is not allowed to run what will the future be for the Brazilian left?

It's really bad to talk about politics based on names. Politics should be discussed related to programs, not individual names. How are they going to govern this country independently of names?

I don't think there will be direct elections in 2018. The elites who made the Coup in Brazil are not joking around. They sold off all of our pre-salt off-shore oil reserves and took billions out of the public health and education systems. However, they haven't been able to finish pushing through their entire agenda in the year since they took power. Furthermore, they don't have a candidate capable of beating anyone from the left. If Lula doesn't run, it will be Ciro Gomes, Jacques Wagner, Fernando Haddad or Eduardo Suplicy. It will be someone who will beat them because they can no longer hide their unpopular agenda. Their agenda is more privatizations, a minimal state, more hunger and lower wages. They are trying to pass a new law in Congress reducing the lunch break to 30 minutes- this is an example of their agenda. They can't hide it anymore. The Brazilian people already know what is going on. One year from now the Brazilian worker who did not take to the streets to fight against the labor law reforms is going to know how much his absence cost. The rejection level against this group who made the Coup and are governing Brazil is already above

90% and is only going to rise. So independently of whether it is Lula or Ciro Gomes, independently of the name, the Brazilian left would win the next election. But in my opinion this won't happen in 2018. I believe that they will try to change the political system to parliamentarism and Congress will appoint Temer as Prime Minister because he is the only guy who has made a total commitment to the Brazilian elite's agenda. It's not just the poor who are furious with the agenda that Temer and his organized crime group are trying to implement. The Brazilian middle class can't take it anymore. The Brazilian middle class is seeing that it entered into a hole and was robbed when it came out in favor of Dilma's impeachment. The nationalist business class realize now that they entered a thievery scheme. It is no longer just the poor, it's everyone who is losing out right now- nearly the entire country is losing. Latin America in general is being deconstructed to recuperate the US power that was lost in the 21st Century. It started losing power over Brazil in the 3rd year of Lula's first mandate when Lula helped strengthen Mercosur, when Brazil let go of its dependence on the US and started spreading out through the rest of the World and strengthening other countries in Latin America. When the Kirchner family and Venezuela agreed to start strengthening Mercosur, it was a defeat for North American imperialism. The growth of China and its entrance in the BRICS was another blow to US hegemony, especially when the BRIC nations decided to create a development bank to rival the World Bank. The Coup that these rotten conservatives brought to Brazil is putting a stop to all this. It's no joke, and it can't be consolidated in one year. This is why I believe there won't be elections in 2018. But I think that Lula should run for office anyway he can. He could run for office from behind bars and he would still win. If the conservatives arrest Lula he will become a hero. If they kill him, he'll become a martyr. And if they leave him alone he'll be the next President of the Republic. There is no way out for the Brazilian right. Their only way out is to continue with the Coup. This is why I don't think there will be elections next year. If they hold elections Lula could win from inside or outside of the prison. If he decides not to run anyone he supports will win the election. And this worries me because nobody is talking about a political project for Brazil anymore. Everyone is just talking about names. And the urban reform movement loses out with this.

Why?

Here is something Lula is saying that I don't agree with. He is saying that if he is elected he'll hold a referendum to ask the Brazilian people if he should annul all of Temer's reforms. In saying this he treats the Coup government as if it were legitimate. You do not need a referendum to annul the actions of an illegitimate government. The Temer government is corrupt and it was put into power illegally through a corrupt congress and judiciary. So you don't have to ask the Brazilian people if you should annul a retrogression in Brazilian labor rights or not. You have to just cancel it, the same way they should annul what the Temer government did to urban policy. This has to be done immediately. The first action that Lula or anyone else should do upon being directly elected to the presidency is to annul everything that the Coup government did in Brazil. They can't just tiptoe around trying to decide if they should punish the bandits or not, like Lula and Dilma did on the issue of the assassins from the Military Dictatorship who killed thousands of workers. We can't start another 13 years of debate over whether we should arrest them or not, as they did with the military dictatorship criminals. We have to be clear with the Brazilian people that to elect Lula is to annul all of the actions of the Coup government. What were their acts? Ending labor rights and taking money away from the poor population's health, education, sanitation and housing programs. This all has to be annulled. Annul everything they gave away to the North American imperialists, like our petroleum. Give the Brazilian people their retirement pensions back. Dilma's allocation of profits from petroleum to pensions, public education and health which the Coup government removed was the best bet to improve quality of life for the Brazilian working class. When Lula says that he's not going to annul everything but will have a referendum, he is recognizing an illegitimate government that took power to sell off our national sovereignty.

There is a large segment of youth on the peripheries who don't seem to understand ultra-conservative candidate Jair Bolsonaro's agenda, who support him against their own best interests. What is your opinion of this?

I think that fascism in Brazil is increasing, this is a fact. And it's not just growing among the rich, its gaining popularity with the poor. We have a repressed agenda in Brazil. The Afro-Brazilian rights agenda and the woman's rights agenda are repressed. The Lula and Dilma governments addressed these two agendas, but they did it in a timid manner. They moved very timidly on the issue of decriminalizing abortion but it moved forward a bit. When they started putting poor kids in rich people's universities through the affirmative action and PROUNI programs, however, this triggered a lot of class hatred. But in my opinion Jair Bolsonaro is being used by the elites. They built him up but, starting in January, I believe the right will begin to attack him too because the PSDB party doesn't see how it can fit into the presidential dispute yet. It looks like Governor Alckmin from São Paulo is going to be their candidate but if you look at the elections there is going to be the PSDB on one side, with whoever it can get in its coalition, and Temer's PMDB party on the other, because anyone who thinks Temer isn't going to run (if they have elections) is fooling himself. Temer will have more support from the center than Alckmin. So we will have Temer, Alckmin and Bolsonaro fighting with each other to make it to the second round against Lula. The left will have three or four candidates, Manuela D'Avila from the PC do B, Ciro Gomes, PSOL will have a candidate so that their party doesn't lose funding and so they can increase their number of congressmen. So there will be four candidates from the left against four from the right: Marina Silva, Bolsonaro, Alckmin and Temer. There will be 8 or 9 people fighting to make it to the second round. The PSDB party does not identify with Bolsonaro, they are interested in electing themselves. Bolsonaro is going to start out 2018 getting punched from the left and the right. It will be just like what's happened to Marina Silva. Who ever thought Marina was going to make it to the second round in 2014? Only people who didn't understand how our elections work. When the game kicked off, PMDB and PSDB played hard to knock down Marina. They will use the same strategy against Bolsonaro. The only thing new is that the PMDB will have its first presidential candidate in 20 years.

We see that the strikes and street protests that have been going on since the Coup are not generating the results that they used to. The unions don't have the membership that they used to because of automation. Capital's influence over the social media, as the BBC recently pointed out, through use of right wing social media robot accounts has influenced the population into supporting politicians who don't support their best interests. What will happen to the future of the Brazilian left, including the social movements, if the elections are canceled next year?

I think that the street protests will increase. I agree with something [Liberation Theology priest and author] Frei Betto recently said. "The people don't know what a Coup is. If the people understood what a Coup is, there wouldn't be enough streets to hold them." Every day that passes as the people discover what a Coup is they will start to mobilize and take it to the streets. It's the Brazilian people who will defeat the Coup, not an election. This is the feeling that the fireman in Brasilia who recently tried to drive his truck into the Congress building experienced. The people have to defend him because he is going to be arrested when he gets out of the hospital. This feeling is growing. The feeling expressed is in the Gabriel o

Pensador song, "Let's kill the president". This feeling is beginning to spread into the favelas and the Brazilian periphery. So the protests are going to grow. When the construction worker leaves his job and the employer screws him over and doesn't pay what he is owed, he will learn what the Coup really means. When he goes into the labor court the next day to sue for what they owe him and he discovers that, due to Temer's labor reforms, he no longer has free legal representation and will be held accountable for all courts costs if he loses to the employer's army of lawyers, he will realize that labor justice has been destroyed in Brazil. When the worker begins to discover this he'll take to the streets to say that labor reforms have to be annulled. So the protests are going to grow. 2018 is going to be a year with a lot of protests and a lot of people on the streets. It will be like the *Direitas Já* movement which brought down the military dictatorship. When it started there were just a few people on the streets. People joked that we weren't large enough to fill a VW Microbus. But we filled the microbus, then we filled full-sized buses then we filled the streets and we won our rights by fighting on the streets. The Coup is going to end with people on the streets. The protests are only going to grow.

Avanildo Duque:
Brazilian NGOs and progressive political action

By Brian Mier

When Brazilians talk about the organized left, they usually refer to the social movements, labor unions and the organic intellectuals who support them. There is another category of civil society, however, that has a positive influence on advances in Brazilian society, the non-governmental organizations, or NGOs. Over the past few decades a number of progressive Brazilian NGOs managed to successfully pilot strategies for poverty alleviation and insert them in public policy and several of these initiatives were duplicated by other governments around the developing world. During the 1980s, the Catholic Church's liberation theology movement had a big impact in the formation of some of Brazil's best NGOs. In Recife, Bishop Dom Hélder Camara, who is famous for saying, "When I feed the poor they call me a saint. When I ask why people are poor, they call me a communist", founded and financed many organizations that are still active to this day. In Rio de Janeiro, NGOs that were originally funded by dioceses connected to the liberation theology movement, such as FASE and IBASE, were influential in founding the World Social Forum. Unfortunately, times have changed in the Brazilian NGO community and many of the country's best organizations are now on the verge of bankruptcy. First, during the 1990s, conservatives within the Catholic Church led by Cardinal Joseph Ratzinger, who later went on to become Pope Benedict XIV, punished key liberation theologians and cut off funding. Then in 2011 when the UN removed Brazil from the World Hunger map and announced that Brazil was on the verge of eliminating extreme poverty most international aid organizations that supported Brazilian NGOs left the country. It's important to remember the influence that NGOs had on the Brazilian left, however, because it forms an integral part of the story of how the nation nearly eliminated hunger and extreme poverty and moved 50 million people into the middle class during the first decade of the 21st Century. This is a success story that was minimized by the commercial northern media during its master narrative change from 2013-2016 during the lead up to the Coup, in which it began portraying Brazil as a failed state. The Northern media seems intent on continuing to downplay this, as evidenced by the recent attention companies like *Bloomberg* have given to a flawed study published by the *World Wealth and Income Database*, which argues that Brazil's inequality reduction was exaggerated based on a disproportionate reliance on income tax return data, in a country in which only 15% of the citizens, those who make over R$2000/year, file income tax returns.

In order to recuperate some of the history of how progressive NGOs contributed to record poverty reduction in Brazil during the PT party governments, I spoke with Avanildo Duque. Mr. Duque grew up in a poor household in the rural Northeast and, against all odds, managed to get degrees in agronomy and geography from the Federal University of Pernambuco. He became an important member of the agro-ecology movement as part of the *Articulação no Semiárido* movement (Semiarid Movement Network/ASA) which was created to develop new strategies for dealing with drought. He currently works as the programs manager for ActionAid Brazil. Active in the women's and LGBT rights movement for decades, in 2017, the women's magazine *Claudia*, elected him as the most feminist man in Brazil.

Recife has some of the most effective and innovative civil society organizations in the World. What are the local characteristics of Recife and Pernambuco that created the conditions for so many good non-governmental organizations to develop there?

I believe that this is the result of two factors. The first is that Recife has a long history of struggle and confrontation led by a progressive left. At the moment of the military Coup of 1964, for example, we had a socialist state government headed by Miguel Arraes that supported the popular education methodology pioneered by fellow Pernambucano Paulo Freire. Pernambuco also had a tradition of the *Ligas Camponensas*, (the Peasants' Leagues) which fought for agrarian reform and were strong before the Coup. So Recife has a progressive tradition that created the conditions to motivate a lot of people to defend citizenship and human rights. Furthermore, we had a very strong liberation theology movement here. Dom Hélder Camara, the Bishop of Recife and Olinda, created various structures within the church that subsequently transformed into NGOs. *CENDEC* (Centro Dom Hélder Camera/Dom Hélder Camara Center) is an example of one of these which is still around today. The *Centro Nordestino de Medicina Popular* (Northeastern People's Medicine Center) is another one, and there are other NGOs that were either started directly by the Catholic Church or were influenced indirectly, such as many NGOs connected to the agro-ecology movement, which received a lot of support from the dioceses. A third factor is indirectly related to the first. There were a lot of people exiled from Recife during the military dictatorship. These people left but they kept their connections to Recife and they started building various organizations while they were still in exile. To give you an idea, most people who were exiled started by moving to Chile and after the Coup there they moved to Europe, especially Germany, France and Switzerland. While in exile some important women activists from Recife began to interact with the European feminist movements. When they were allowed to return home, they joined with women who were still here and created a new women's' social movement that created three important feminist NGOs. 30 years later two of them are still around and are among the best of their kind in Brazil. The first is *SOS Corpo* (SOS Body) which grew out of the need for women to discuss sexual and reproductive rights. The second is *Casa da Mulher do Nordeste* (Northeastern Women's House) which grew out of the need for women to have economic autonomy. The fourth and final factor that I will mention here is that, due to international relationships within the progressive sectors of the Catholic Church and citizenship rights organizations, many international development agencies began to view Recife as a reference for the non-governmental sector and began to set up permanent offices here. By the 1990s and early oughties, Recife was full of offices from organizations like OXFAM, GTZ (The German Technical Cooperation Agency), and CARITAS.

What role did the NGO sector play during the 13 years of PT party governments in Brazil?

When the process of political opening began during the final years of the dictatorship, the formation of the PT party played a major role for the left. I wouldn't say that the NGOs had the most important role in the rebirth of the Brazilian left at the time. The fact is that the labor union movement, MST and the Catholic Pastorals, along with remnants of the old left political parties that were re-legalized and came in as competitors to the PT, were the most important factors, but there was a contribution that also cannot be belittled made by the civil society organizations that we now call NGOs. Here in Recife, people like Adelmo Araujo made important contributions in the structuring of the PT party as organic intellectuals who had an important influence in terms of building political platforms and bridged an alignment, that was sometimes a bit complicated, with academics. So they had an influence on the creation of the PT party and its arrival in power. When the PT disputed and almost won the 1989 elections many organizations were preparing to create a left government, which at the time was much farther left than the government that eventually took power when Lula won in 2003. After the 1989 elections the PT created a parallel government platform along with other left parties. Civil society organizations contributed through the accumulation of local experiences and pilot projects on the various themes that they worked on. One of the best examples - and something that I participated in - comes from the field of agriculture. There was an interesting dynamic between the Marxists, who supported an egalitarian distribution of the means of production in agriculture, and a group of progressive agronomists who were more focused on the organic, sustainable agriculture movement. So there were two perspectives that dialogued within the process of building priorities within the PT during the 1990s that influenced policy later when Lula started building his government in 2003. The PT party recognized the agro-ecological NGOs as strategic partners but in my evaluation they were unable to create a full counter-hegemony. The unions, the social movements and the liberation theology branch of the church were more influential on the formation of Lula's government, despite the fact that they hired many people from the NGO field. To give you an idea I was invited to join Lula's agricultural team 4 times. I didn't accept the offers, partially because of personal reasons but also because I had my doubts about the project they were building due to the electoral coalitions that I thought were very complicated. But I know a lot of people who entered the government at that time and remained there for over a decade contributing their expertise to its programs. Without a doubt, they developed some interesting programs that greatly reduced rural poverty. I will give an example of development in the semi-arid region of the Northeast, the drought-plagued region that traditionally had the highest poverty levels. Before the Lula government, while FHC was president, we created a coalition of NGOs called the *Articulação do Semiárido* (Semi-Arid Articulation/ASA). It was a network that linked NGOs with rural workers unions and Catholic Church organizations spread through the 10 states in Brazil that have semi-arid biomes. The ASA built a proposal to adapt to the semi-arid biome that radically transformed the vision that we have about droughts. Historically, you could say that the phenomenon of droughts were treated in a positivist manner, based on climactic determinism. For generations this led to policies that were designed to "fight" the droughts, within the historic rural political system, called *colonialismo*, that concentrated water in the hands of the elite ranchers and plantation owners, which in turn increased the concentration of land and power. We started a dialogue explaining that were other ways of thinking about the semi-arid biome, that droughts were a recurrent climactic phenomenon and that we had enough knowledge of their cycles and social technologies to prepare for them in advance, not to just react to them after the fact as natural emergencies because emergency response continually strengthened the rich and increased the concentration of power. The traditional emergency response strategy involved rural laborers working for very low salaries on big public works projects to accumulate water, typically on the private property of local political families who would exploit the local population during droughts. ASA began saying, "No. We have to think of the Semi-arid region as an area that has periodic droughts in which the people should have knowledge on how to minimize risks and prepare for them". ASA built a ten state wide network of disseminating what we now call social technologies for accumulating water and decentralizing water management. Rain water capture through cisterns was the main tool, but together with the construction of these family and village cisterns there was a whole dialogue about the importance of water management and decentralization and the importance of thinking of ways to increase the kinds of agriculture and animal husbandry that work best in this kind of biome. The Lula administration went on to incorporate this into federal government policy and built 1 million family rain waters cisterns in the semi arid region. So today we can say that the paradigm of coexistence with the semi-arid climate prevailed. There has been this 15 year experience of installing rain water capture technology which goes beyond the systems themselves to include discussions about natural resource management, peoples' autonomy and the possibility of living well in this environment and this caused huge improvement in quality of life for millions of people. Obviously this process was greatly strengthened by two federal government policies implemented by the PT government. The first policy was the large, above inflation level minimum wage increases which also increased the retirement pensions for rural workers which provided retired family farmers and laborers in the semi-arid region with capital to stimulate the local economy. The second factor that contributed to millions of rural workers rising above the poverty line in the semi-arid region was the *bolsa familia* income redistribution program which, although it was very timid from my point of view, made an extraordinary difference in the region, especially when combined with the social technologies that were pioneered by the ASA network. When these factors were combined, millions of people in what was once Brazil's poorest region rose above the poverty line. You can see the results the last drought, which was considered one of the worst in Brazilian history. For the first time anyone can remember we didn't have riots, looting and mass internal migration. Up until the 1990s, every time there was a big drought people would loot to avoid starving to death. There was a lot of death. Infant mortality rates in the region were very high due to the food insecurity caused by the droughts and by diseases caused by poor water quality and this caused a huge exodus to other regions of Brazil which resulted in cities like São Paulo and Rio de Janeiro seeing 500% population increases during the second half of the 20th century and a resulting exponential increase in favelas. This scenario changed drastically but we see now, with the change in government caused by the institutional *Coup d'Etat*, that we are running the risk of regressing back to old paradigm of the drought industry. We saw this during last round of municipal elections in the rural northeast where the federal government, instead of strengthening the *Agua para Todos* (Water for Everyone) program with its cisterns and other technologies, hired water trucks for its favorite candidates to go house to house giving away water as if it were a favor. In conclusion, this is a specific example in which Brazilian NGOs made a very important contribution to reducing poverty. They didn't act alone but they made a big contribution to moving sound public policies forwards in the region.

How did Recife's feminist NGOs contribute to advancing women's policies during the PT years?

Evaluating the situation coolly, Brian, I don't think that the women's movement managed to influence the PT governments very much, even with the first woman president in office. Despite the PT creating the first national Women's Ministry, which strengthened the dialogue on women's rights, it was very marginalized in terms of budget and autonomy to define policies. If we analyze this period there was some progress for women but these advances don't correspond with the intensity of the Brazilian women's and feminist movements. We didn't succeed in transforming many of the programs into official state policy and some of them that were approved during this period, such as the *Maria da Penha* domestic violence law, were very difficult to implement because there weren't enough resources allocated to them. I believe we lost a big opportunity to move forwards on fundamental women's rights issues during this period. In terms of women's representation in political office, the PT party was unable to move forwards with a political reform to guarantee gender equity, despite this being one of the top priorities of the women's movement. Today Brazil is ranked 115th out of 138 countries in terms of gender equity in political office. In terms of women's rights I believe there were more lost opportunities than victories during the PT years.

My next question is for Avanildo, the person, not the NGO director. You grew up as the poor son of a market vendor in Paulo Afonso, Bahia. You are black, gay and northeastern. In other words, you stand for everything that Jair Bolsonaro and his neo-fascist minions hate. Through your job, you interact a lot with poor young people in Brazil. How do you explain the rise of the far right among the poor and working class and what can be done to fight this tendency?

This is a complex question since it is personal, as you say. First of all we've only experienced a few short periods of democracy in Brazil, and during these periods the democracy that we had was fragile. I think we just ended a practice period with the state as a guarantor of rights that, timidly, was moving forwards. The other thing is that for the vast majority of our history we have had very violent regimes. Our country was founded through the total devastation of the Indian's common goods, the importation of monoculture cycles and natural resource appropriation for the benefit of Europe. We then imported an entire patriarchal foundation from the Middle Ages including the Inquisition and its courts and slavery. Brazil was built in a very violent manner against the native population, the African slaves and against women. It was also very violent in terms of class because from the beginning a feudal culture was imposed, first with the slaves and then with the rural laborers after slavery ended, with peasants feeding into labor force during the industrialization process. Consequently we have a very strong conservative, elitist, racist and patriarchal heritage. In the brief moments when Democracy arrived here, in this cycle of periodic democracy in Brazil, we haven't managed to build policies to counter this. The explicit return of the far right is generated by two factors. Firstly, because of our extreme conservative heritage, and secondly because the last progressive government did not use education as a tool for liberation. In terms of education, the government was orthodox and pragmatic within the capitalist structure and was much more concerned with increasing incomes, employment, production and the GDP, and much less with strengthening education as a possibility for pedagogical deconstruction of these traditional pillars within Brazilian society. Nevertheless, the few changes that we achieved, some of which were significant in the history of Brazil such as affirmative action, generated class hatred that was incensed by the media. The PT party made a strategic error in aligning with the evangelical churches for electoral purposes. The Coup was orchestrated by the elites who were angry that the PT extended land rights to the *quilombola* communities and the landless peasants, despite the fact that this could have been done more aggressively. Brazil's exit from the world hunger map and migration of 50 million people into the middle classes filled them with fear of losing their privileges, so they developed a project to take back the power. They returned with an entire culture of hate, fed by other institutional powers like the judiciary, that fomented racism, sexism, and homophobia and naturalized the extermination of poor youth. I think the violence comes from long ago and the few advances that we had in terms of political rights during the PT governments generated a huge amount of hatred against people with my profile as you pointed out in your question. Hatred against different groups of people is now in fashion, including against people here in the northeast, whose lives greatly improved during the PT years. The redistributive measures may have been timid but for a while we were actually reducing income inequality. The GINI coefficient may have only improved slightly but this was unacceptable for the Brazilian elites, who are the historic beneficiaries of slavery, patriarchy and class exploitation.

Today in Brazil many of the most respected NGOs are running the risk of bankruptcy. The social movements have an aging membership. The unions have lost a lot of members due to things like automation, computers and robots. In a context in which the traditional pillars of the Brazilian left are weakened compared to 2002, how can the Brazilian people mobilize in 2018 to undo the Coup?

This Coup was very well built. The first strategy was to beat Dilma in the 2014 elections. It didn't work. Immediately afterwords, Eduardo Cunha, the president of Congress and Aécio Neves, the Senate President, led a strategy to paralyze the government. Dilma reacted by giving into conservative demands and agreeing to enact moderate reforms in an attempt to hold onto power, but the more she conceded the more inevitable it became. Working in tandem, the media and the judiciary launched an objective strategy to take control over the state and political hegemony. We saw the sudden, suspicious and apparently criminal death of one of the Supreme Court Justices and his replacement by someone who is totally unqualified from a judicial point of view, who was the Minister of Justice in this corrupt Coup government. Then we had a vindictive, partisan federal judge and prosecutor lead a totally biased persecution against Lula, and a new Federal Police director took power who is totally committed to this corrupt government. Along with these changes came a loss of rights - one after another. The process continues and we are losing one human right after another, in total disrespect to the federal constitution, through economic reforms carried out in the name of the rentier capital that is represented by this government. This creates a huge challenge for the left because we resisted as much as we could against the Coup. Symbolically, Dilma deserves credit for not resigning or turning over her mandate until the very end. But it is a scenario of aging, weakened and fragmented social movements in the face of worsening structural adjustments, with the most progressive and combative movements such as the MST unable to give an effective response. Since the Coup was very quick, the capacity to create dialogue and a response from the left was limited and the sequence of defeats which we are all suffering from is demobilizing resistance and weakening the chances for a more progressive government to take power. The left doesn't have many options today. I think it's a bad indicator that we have to bet on the candidacy of Lula as a possibility to rescue some of the rights we lost in the last year. It is a sign that we have been unable to build a successor on the left. And this succession is the responsibility of PT and Lula - they were not able to do this. I think that the choice of Dilma was incorrect because we had other perspectives and could have created a better field of possibilities. So today, the idea that betting on Lula is our best chance is a bad sign because it shows lack of renovation and a renewable program on the left. On the other hand Dilma said something astute in an interview last week. She said that the right doesn't have any strong candidates, "Because if it did, it wouldn't have to work so hard to try to invalidate Lula's candidacy". If the right had a strong candidate it would be calm, letting the communications companies and governmental apparatus guarantee the victory of its candidate. In this vacuum on the right, Jair Bolsonaro steps in, but he is more of a populist than a neoliberal. Bolsonaro's entire campaign strategy is basically just being against the PT. And he has a neo-fascist agenda that is resonating with the youth on the periphery who are living in a climate of religious fundamentalism. It's a complicated scenario but I don't think it is favoring either side, because there are all kinds of possibilities now. There is only 10 months until the elections - if they have them – so there isn't enough time to build another Fernando Collor. Some sectors of the right find it disagreeable to have to bet on someone like Jair Bolsonaro. I think it is a complex situation and there are two elements that will affect the outcome. The first is the extremely unpopular retirement reforms. If they pass, there will be such a backlash against the government that it may end up trying to cancel the elections in an attempt to hold onto power and this will strengthen the left. Another factor is the youth and the alternative and social media, which are taking an increasingly important role. They were important in consolidating of the Coup. The right is more structured for active communications in these mediums and I think the social media represents a false democratization of access to information. Nevertheless, the left has to develop a more aggressive media strategy because it is a field of dispute that is very important, that influences elections all over the world. I do not think that, in the current conjuncture, the social movements, unions and NGOs have the power to generate a counter-hegemony. They have an important responsibility, however, to rethink their reason for existence in the current scenario. They need to reflect on their design, structure and dynamics in this current period which I refer to as a period of losses. If we don't apply what we've learned from these losses to think how we can survive and resist and create political renewal, when the tides do begin to turn we will be weaker than before. Therefore, the upcoming election is an important moment but it's more important to reflect on the roles of the NGOs and the social movements so that that we don't fade away, so that we can continue to resonate as much as possible, so that when a more favorable moment comes along we can return with a greater capacity for action than what we are seeing now. This is my humble, analytical contribution.

Communist Presidential Candidate Manuela D'Avila:
The fight to guarantee that the 2018 elections happen

By Brian Mier

The *Partido Comunista do Brasil* (PC do B/Communist Party of Brazil) was founded in 1962 when a group of militants split from the older *Partido Comunista Brasileiro* (PCB/Brazilian Communist Party). It was criminalized during the Military Dictatorship and as communists were arrested, tortured and executed, 80 party members moved to the remote Amazon region of Araguaia and started an anti-fascist guerrilla war that lasted 7 years, was completely censored in the Brazilian media, and required 5000 Brazilian army troops to repress. As the military dictatorship came to an end, a process of political opening enabled the party to regain its legal status. It reformulated itself as a Marxist party that supported radical structural reform over revolution. Since then, it has maintained status as one of the larger leftist Brazilian political parties. In a nation which ranks among the World's worst in terms of gender equity among elected officials, it is the party that has come the closest to achieving it. Along with the smaller *Partido Socialismo e Liberdade* (Socialism and Liberty Party/PSOL), it made up part of the Lula and Dilma Rousseff governments' inner coalition in Congress, voting together with the PT party on nearly everything. The PC do B currently has 12 elected congressmen and women, one senator, 80 mayors and controls the state of Maranhão, where governor Flavio Dino created the highest public teacher salaries in the nation and issued a decree to remove all names of military dictatorship officials from public streets, schools and monuments.

Manuela D'Avila, 36, is the PC do B party candidate for the presidency in 2018 and the first Communist presidential candidate in Brazil since 1945. A journalist who rose up within the *União Nacional dos Estudantes* (National Students Union/ UNE), she first entered the political stage as the youngest city councilor in Porto Alegre history in 2004. There, she created and drafted a law giving students the right to pay half for entrance fees to movies, cultural and sporting events. In 2007, she was elected to Congress with the highest number of votes in her state, Rio Grande do Sul. There, in 2011, she presented and ratified the Youth Statute - a law that defines teenagers' rights and the government's responsibilities to them, which was criticized by evangelical pastors at the time for its language guaranteeing LGBT rights.

You are the first communist Brazilian Presidential candidate since Yedo Fiúza ran for office in 1945, for the Partida Comunista Brasileiro *(Brazilian Communist Party/PCB). How has the concept of communism changed in Brazil since those days? Does your platform still have anything in common with Fiúza's?*

In the last 70 years? Wow, we have certainly had significant changes in the international communist movement during this period, and our party is no different. I think the biggest challenges to the communist movement in history have taken place since 1945. On the one hand we are the heirs to the construction of the international and Brazilian communist movements. On the other hand there have been profound changes. The most important difference is that today we believe in building our own experiences to create a Brazilian kind of socialism that is not based on any models.

What is the PC do B's position related to capitalism?

We are a political party that understands that capitalism generates inequality and does not enable people to live in the best way that they can.

In your opinion, what were some of the things that the PT party governments of Lula and Dilma got right and where did they make mistakes? How does your plan for governance differ from that of Lula's?

The PT governments got a lot of things right. They deeply transformed the country, brought millions of people out of extreme poverty and, for the first time ever, guaranteed a sovereign foreign policy. But they didn't manage to push through the reforms that were so important to guarantee the structural transformation of the Brazilian state. We didn't enact political reform, we didn't reform the media laws and we didn't have urban reform or tax code reform. So we failed to enact the big reforms.

The PC do B is the second largest true left political party in Brazil. Unlike the PSOL party, PC do B has full national support from a social movement, the Confederação Nacional das Associações de Moradores *(National Residents Association Confederation/CONAM) and a labor union federation, the* Central dos Trabalhadores e Trabalhadoras do Brasil *(Workers Central of Brazil/CTB). Together they have around 1 million members who will certainly take to the streets to campaign for you next year, but both organizations are not as strong as they used to be. How can you use this historic moment for the PC do B, of launching its first presidential candidate ever, to re-energize the party base?*

We will revitalize both our base and the Brazilian people's struggle through a national development project. We think that confronting these ultra-conservative *golpistas* (putschists) who are taking away the people's basic human rights will guarantee the support and enthusiasm of the people.

Since last year's Coup, there have been huge general strikes and street protests but the government continues to remove all kinds of basic human rights from the people (for example law 13.465/17, passed in October, which makes it harder to prosecute big plantation owners for stealing indigenous lands). Now there are a lot of people who are saying that the Coup government is going to try to cancel next year's presidential elections. How can the left reorganize and mobilize to remove these rentiers from power, with or without elections next year?

Our biggest fight at the moment is to guarantee that the 2018 elections actually happen. Our strategy is based on resistance and perspective. We have to resist against the daily attacks on our rights, such as the attacks on labor rights and the retirement pension reforms. As we resist, we have to organize to guarantee that we can dispute the future of Brazil in direct presidential elections in 2018.

Conclusion

By Brian Mier

This book represents the culmination of 22 years living in Brazil and interacting with people from the Brazilian organized left, both as a development professional and as an activist journalist. The questions asked in the unstructured interviews, as well as in the background research I provided for the interviews conducted by Al Jazeera's *The Listening Post,* were based on my learning through this long process of participant observation. The interviewees represent a cross section of the Brazilian organized left that is geographically skewed. Eight interviewees are from the Southeast; two are from the South; two are from the Northeast; two are from the North and none are from the Midwest, a region that is not known for having a strong organized left. Four of the 14 interviewees are female, and, in a country which is 54% black, four interviewees are people of color. The geographical disparity is a result of my prioritizing personal interviews with people who live near me in the Brazilian Southeast, over phone, skype or email. Gender and ethnic disparities reflect my failure to give enough attention to these issues while organizing the interviews, historic inequalities in opportunity, and a failure of leadership in the unions, social movements and professions to correct these disparities. When taken in a context of near total lack of voices from the Brazilian organized left in the Northern media, however, the fact that this group of interviews is being published in English is a victory in itself. Hopefully it will lead to more pressure on northern news companies to provide the right of response in their reporting, through seeking out representatives of the large percentage of the Brazilian population that supports left political parties.

I am not affiliated with any Brazilian political party. I supported PT candidate Lula in 2002, PSOL candidate Heloisa Helena in 2006, PSOL candidate Plinio Arruda in 2010, and PT candidate Dilma Rousseff in 2014. Why, a reader might ask, have so many of the interviewees in this book expressed support for the PT Party? Why haven't I given equal time to supporters of PSOL? In my opinion the PSOL Party and its supporters, comprised of around 1.5% of the Brazilian electorate, already have a disproportionate amount of representation in northern academia and alternative media. This representation has led to misunderstandings about the Brazilian left abroad. I do respect the PSOL Party, however.

I would like to draw a few conclusions about the Brazilian political context based on my analysis of the interviews that appear in this book.

The first is that Dilma Rousseff's impeachment can rightfully be called a Coup. There was a unanimous consensus among the interviewees about this point. Furthermore supporting evidence continues to roll in, most recently the October 17, 2017 revelations in *Folha de São Paulo*, that impeachment architect and jailed former Congressional President Eduardo Cunha received funding from a prominent stock broker and paid it to members of Congress in exchange for votes to impeach Dilma Rousseff [i]. This represents an alternative viewpoint to the hegemonic northern media, which worked to legitimize the illegal impeachment process from start to finish. Even so-called "liberal" commercial publications, such as the The Guardian, ran articles justifying the legality of the impeachment process. This occurred despite the fact that fiscal peddling, the accusation that triggered the Rousseff impeachment, (of which Rousseff was later declared innocent), is not an impeachable offense in Brazil [ii][iii]. As Gegê da Silva, national leader of the *Central de Movimentos Populares* (Popular Movements Central, CMP), says, "There is not a shadow of a doubt that what happened in Brazil was a coup.

And it's a coup that continues to be enacted on a daily basis on the backs of the working class" [iv].

Manipulation in the Brazilian media was a critical factor in laying the groundwork for the coup. In his interview, Paulo Henrique Amorim says, "Globo is the first and most powerfull power in this country. It's more important than the political parties and more important than the church. Currently the Editor in Chief for the evening news at Globo is the most powerful politician in this country." As documented by interviewee João Feres in his *Manchetometro* project, which quantifies media bias, the Brazilian media oligarchies continue to support the coup government on a daily basis as they set back decades of advances in human, environmental and labor rights. Carlos Latuff's metaphor of a pig in a tank, shooting a newspaper gun out of a television, is a perfect metaphor for the role played by the Brazilian media. Far too often, lazy or underpaid foreign correspondents take stories from Brazil's conservative media at face value, and use them as primary sources for English language articles about Brazil (as I documented in Brasil Wire regarding the New York Times and Washington Post's use of Veja magazine) [v].

The new coup government is working to destroy what was left of Brazilian developmentalism. The two PT governments attempted to balance supporting neoliberal central bank policies of their predecessors while implementing developmentalist policies, based on the theories of Raul Prebisch and Celso Furtado. This included minimum wage increases and subsidies for internal industrial production, consumption, and other key sectors of the economy such as the construction industry. In doing so, Lula bet on a strong petit-bourgeois national business elite. Key businesses controlled by this class in the petroleum, shipbuilding, and construction industries were completely paralyzed during the *Lava Jato* investigation, causing the Brazilian economy to implode. Some economists estimated that the recession was 300% deeper than it would have been without *Lava Jato* [vi]. Economic activities in Brazil's largest companies were paralyzed and their owners, unlike most politicians involved, were systematically jailed until they agreed to plea bargain their way out (represented at times by prosecutor and *Lava Jato* judge Sergio Moro's wife's law firm) [vii]. Meanwhile, Northern capital flooded into these sectors, parts of which are now controlled by parties who have no vested interest in Brazil [vii]. As Erminia Maricato says, "The cycle of a strong nationalist business class has come to an end" [ix].

Changes in the Brazilian political economy have both weakened workers' ability to organize and weakened support for a nationalist development project. As MST leader Gilmar Mauro says, "There are structural changes underway in the world political economy that are eroding the left's traditional organizational tactics and there is a growing segment of workers that no longer has space within the capitalist labor structure" [x]. Douglas Izzo, São Paulo President of the CUT Union Federation, observes that robotics and computerization caused the number of factory and other historically unionized Brazilian jobs such as bank tellers to plummet. In the early 1980s, the CUT had 18 million members. Today it has 8 million, while productive output of industries like metallurgy has increased [xi]. Even traditional jobs in the service sector are disappearing. The MST's Gilmar Mauro says, "Today the largest taxi company in the world doesn't own one car. The largest hotel company in the world doesn't own one room" [xii]. There is a huge increase in the number of autonomous workers who receive no benefits or job security in Brazil, thanks to companies like Uber. This situation will be vastly exacerbated due to Michel Temer's draconian labor rights reforms [xiii]. Consequently, the traditional left tactic of the strike is losing force. Although the largest general strike in Latin America this century took place in Brazil on April 28, 2017, it did not succeed in halting the labor law reforms [xiv].

In an atmosphere in which grassroots organizing and other traditional leftist tactics such as strikes and street protests were weakened, and no viable alternative to the PT party emerged, the organized left created two inter-related civil society coalitions, the *Frente Brasil Popular* (Popular Brazil Front, FBP) and the *Frente do Povo sem Medo* (Fearless People's Front). Starting during the lead-up to the coup, these groups worked together to stage large street protests and two general strikes. Although some people try to divide them along ideological lines, the largest civil society organizations in both movements are the same: the CUT and the MST. In May 2017, they worked together to organize the largest protest in Brasilia's history, which brought over 200,000 people to the streets and resulted in Congressional president Rodrigo Maia temporarily declaring martial law [xv].

The vast majority of the organized Brazilian left, including the CUT Labor Union Federation and the largest urban and rural social movements, believe the PT party is the only party that currently has a feasible plan to retake the Brazilian Government and to undo the damage that was done over the past year to human rights, the environment, national autonomy, the public health and education systems. This popular support for Lula, as represented in the election poll numbers, seems to represent a pragmatic choice. This is due to a difficult political and economic scenario in which other viable candidates for the presidency range from ultra-neoliberal to neo-fascist. The fact that the organized left continues to support Lula should not be ignored or downplayed by people who are trying to understand the current political context in Brazil. The current two top priorities of the Brazilian organized left are to fight to guarantee that direct elections actually take place, and electing Lula. As the MST's Gilmar Mauro says, "We are confronting power and resisting against setbacks. This is why we support Lula at the moment. We are acting to form resistance, including electing him to the presidency to move forward with social reforms" [xvi].

However, as interviewee Avanildo Duque says, the idea that betting on Lula is our best chance is a bad sign because it shows lack of renovation and a renewable program on the left. What, therefore, can be done? Some suggestions for possible courses of action appear in this book: 1) As Manuela D'avila says, fight to guarantee that direct elections are not canceled in 2018; 2) Take advantage of what Avanildo Duque calls an opportune moment to reflect on strengths and weaknesses and our reason for existence, so that when a new opportunity arises to retake power, we will be stronger than we are today; and 3) Follow people like Erminia Maricato's example and, whether through the *Frente Brasil Popular* or the *Povo Sem Medo*, organize to plan for the kind of society we want in the mid to long term with the understanding that things are going to get worse before they get better.

What can people in the developed world do to strengthen these processes? One step in the right direction would be to question journalists when they don't provide a right of response to people from the organized left in their reporting on Brazil. Another step would be to try to listen to what members of the organized left have to say and prioritize solidarity over criticism.

End Notes

[i] Cunha recebeu R$ 1 Mi para 'comprar' votos do impeachment de Dilma, diz Funaro", October 14, 2017, http://www1.folha.uol.com.br/poder/2017/10/1927138-cunha-recebeu-r-1-mi-para-comprar-votos-do-impeachment-de-dilma-diz-funaro.shtml

[ii] Fabio Fabrini, "Para o ministerio publico, pedaladas do governo de Dilma não são crime", Jornal Estado de São Paulo, July 14, 2016,http://politica.estadao.com.br/noticias/geral,para-mp-pedaladas-do-governo-dilma-nao-sao-crime,10000062862

[iii] Jonathan Watts, "Brazil's Impeachment: What you Need to Know", The Guardian, August 31, 2016, https://www.theguardian.com/news/2016/aug/31/dilma-rousseff-impeachment-brazil-what-you-need-to-know

[iv] Luiz Gonzaga "Gege" da Silva, "The General Strike and the Survival of the Latin American Left", Interview by Brian Mier, COHA, May 16, 2017, http://www.coha.org/the-general-strike-and-the-survival-of-the-latin-american-left-an-interview-with-luiz-gonzaga-gege-da-silva/

[v] Brian Mier, "The Problem with Veja", Brasil Wire, Brasil Wire, August 3, 2015, http://www.brasilwire.com/veja/

[vi] Brian Mier, "How Manufactured Economic Crisis in Brazil Paved the Way for a Soft Coup", Upside Down World, September 25, 2017, http://upsidedownworld.org/archives/brazil/manufactured-economic-crisis-brazil-paved-way-soft-coup/

[vii] Monica Bergamo, "Advogado acusa amigo de Moro de intervir em acordo", Folha de São Paulo, August 27, 2017,

http://www1.folha.uol.com.br/poder/2017/08/1913355-advogado-acusa-amigo-de-moro-de-intervir-em-acordo.shtml

[viii] Pedro Peduzzi, "Shell investeria US$ 10 bilhões na Petrobras e no pre-sal", EBC Agencia Brasil, October 11, 2016, http://agenciabrasil.ebc.com.br/economia/noticia/2016-11/shell-investira-us-10-bilhoes-na-petrobras-e-no-pre-sal

[ix] Erminia Maricato, "Overcoming Deep Inequality in Brazilian Cities", Interview by Brian Mier, COHA, April 24, 2017, http://www.coha.org/overcoming-deep-inequality-in-brazilian-cities-an-interview-with-erminia-maricato/

[x] Gilmar Mauro, "MST and the Fight to Change the Brazilian Power Structure", Interview by Brian Mier, COHA, September 6, 2017, http://www.coha.org/mst-and-the-fight-to-change-the-brazilian-power-structure-an-interview-with-gilmar-mauro/

[xi] Douglas Izzo, "There is No Negotiation Whatsoever", Interview by Brian Mier, COHA, March 17, 2016, http://www.coha.org/there-is-no-negotiation-whatsoever-union-leader-douglas-izzo-talks-about-labor-rights-in-post-coup-brazil/

[xii] Mauro, "MST and the Fight" (see endnote ix)

[xiii] Julia Dolce, "Com desmonte trabalhista, empresas já começam procurar terceirizados e autonomos", Brasil de Fato, August 7, 2017, https://www.brasildefato.com.br/2017/08/07/com-desmonte-trabalhista-empresas-ja-comecam-a-procurar-terceirizados-e-autonomos/

[xiv] "Em casa ou nas ruas, greve geral envolveu 35 milhões de pessoas, dizem organizadores", Rede Brasil Atual, April 28, 2017, http://www.redebrasilatual.com.br/trabalho/2017/04/em-casa-ou-nas-ruas-greve-geral-envolveu-35-milhoes-de-pessoas-dizem-organizadores

[xv] "Ante maior marcha na historia da Brasilia, Temer mostra que é fraco e covarde, diz CUT", Rede Brasil Atual, May 24, 2017, http://www.redebrasilatual.com.br/politica/2017/05/mais-de-200-mil-pessoas-ocuparam-brasilia-contra-reformas-e-por-eleicoes-diretas

[xvi] Mauro, "MST and the Fight" (see endnote ix)